THE "DRUG WAR" IN COLOMBIA

THE NEGLECTED TRAGEDY
OF POLITICAL VIOLENCE

October 1990

An Americas Watch Report

Human Rights Watch
485 Fifth Avenue
New York, NY 10017-6104
Tel (212) 972-8400
Fax (212) 972-0905

Human Rights Watch
1522 K Street, NW, #910
Washington, DC 20005
Tel (202) 371-6592
Fax (202) 371-0124

ISBN 0-929692-48-9
Library of Congress Catalog Card Number: 90-85380

Cover design by Deborah Thomas

Contents

Acknowledgments

This report was written by Juan E. Méndez, Executive Director of Americas Watch, and edited by Kenneth Roth, Deputy Director of Human Rights Watch. Graduate student Karen Plafker and law student Arturo José Carrillo, interns at Americas Watch, contributed the first drafts of Chapters II and VII respectively. Clifford Rohde and Patricia Sinay, of the Washington office of Americas Watch, provided research assistance. Allyson Collins, of Human Rights Watch in Washington, provided research and comments on United States policy. The author gratefully acknowledges comments on early drafts by Jamie Fellner, Juan G. Tokatlian and Gustavo Gallón. Juan E. Méndez visited Bogotá in March 1989 and Bogotá and Barrancabermeja in May 1990, in preparation for this report. Colombian government officials, judges and prosecutors were generous with their time and provided very useful information. Extensive assistance was received from the Andean Commission of Jurists—Colombian Section in making appointments and other arrangements for those fact-finding missions, as well as in answering many legal and factual questions. Finally, Americas Watch wishes to express gratitude to the many human rights monitors in Colombia, not only for the documentation and insight offered for this report, but also for the inspiration provided by their boundless courage.

List of Acronyms

ACDEGAM Peasant Association of Cattlemen and Farmers of the
 Magdalena Medio
ANUC Asociación Nacional de Usuarios Campesinos
CEIS Centro de Estudios e Investigaciones Sociales
CGNSB Coordinadora Guerrillera Simón Bolívar
CINEP Centro de Investigacíon y Educación Popular
CONADHEGS Coordinación Nacional de Derechos Humanos y
 Damnificados por la Guerra Sucia
CSSP Comité de Solidaridad con los Presos Políticos
DAS Departamento Administrativo de Seguridad
DEA U.S. Drug Enforcement Administration
DIJIN Intelligence and Judicial Investigations Bureau of the Police
DNIC Dirección Nacional de Instrucción Criminal
ELN Ejército de Liberación Nacional
EPL Ejécito Popular de Liberación
FARC Fuerzas Armadas Revolucionarias de Colombia
FETRAMETAL metal-workers union
IACHR Inter-American Commission on Human Rights
ICRC International Committee of the Red Cross
INDERENA Institute for Renewable Natural Resources and the
 Environment
M-19 Movimiento 19 de Abril
MAS Muerte a Secuestradores
MRN Muerte a Revolucionarios del Noreste
NACLA North American Conference on Latin America
NCO Non-commissioned Officer
NGO Non-governmental Organization
OAS Organization of American States
OIE Oficina de Investigaciones Especiales
PNR Plan for National Rehabilitation
PRT Partido Revolucionario de los Trabajadores
UP Unión Patriótica

I. Introduction

Political violence in Colombia continues to take more lives than in any other country in the hemisphere. Some of the killings take place during fighting between combatants, but most are cases of simple murder. Those responsible for these murders include members of the military and security forces as well as insurgents, hired gunmen and paramilitary groups. The intellectual authors of these crimes are comparably varied. The very complexity of political violence in Colombia often serves as a shield for those who order and commit violent acts.

As this report demonstrates, the Colombian government has done too little to work through these complexities to identify, prosecute and punish those behind the political violence. This failing has been greatest in acknowledging the role of military and security forces in the killings. These forces continue to commit violent abuses themselves, and to condone and support killings by paramilitary groups.

The problem is most acute in the case of paramilitary groups. These groups, which have been responsible for some of the largest and most sensational massacres, are gangs of highly trained killers, often masquerading as "self-defense" associations of farmers. Powerful economic interests recruit, train, finance and support these bands, and use them to target leftist political activists, leaders of peasant and popular organizations, and those Colombians perceived to be the "social base" of the guerrillas. Drug traffickers are among the most prominent supporters of paramilitary groups, a fact which the Colombian government has seized to blame the so-called Medellín cartel for virtually all political violence in Colombia. Before, during and after the cartel's involvement, however, some wealthy landowners have sponsored such groups.[1]

---

[1] These include cattle breeders and emerald miners in the Magdalena Medio region, banana growers in Urabá, cattlemen in the *Llanos Orientales* (Eastern Plains) and breeders and farmers in the Atlantic Coast departments of Córdoba,

The Colombian government has failed to acknowledge that paramilitary groups could not commit many of their crimes without significant support from certain high-ranking Army officers. These military leaders assist the groups by providing intelligence on the selection of targets, occasionally by giving them weapons, and by protecting them from investigation and prosecution. The Army high command has done nothing to punish these instances of illegal cooperation. To the contrary, it has obstructed the few courageous efforts by civilian authorities to investigate these links.

In April 1989, the government of President Virgilio Barco took an important step toward stopping paramilitary violence by withdrawing legal recognition from "civil defense" associations and making it illegal for the Army to arm them. There is strong evidence, however, that the Army has continued to force peasants to join these groups, under threat of being considered a "guerrilla supporter," with its potentially deadly consequences. The Army has also provided important logistical support in the field. The Barco anti-paramilitary strategy failed to recognize this continuing Army role in paramilitary violence, with the result that most investigative and prosecutorial efforts have focused exclusively on civilian gang members.

This narrow focus was only reinforced by the August 1989 "war on drug trafficking," launched against the Medellín cartel in response to the murder of Senator Luis Carlos Galán, the presidential candidate of the Liberal Party. The government's insistence that the Medellín cartel leaders are responsible for all violent abuses has become a serious obstacle to efforts to halt the violence, since it has left other paramilitary groups largely free to assassinate leftist leaders and massacre their perceived supporters.[2]

Cesar and Sucre.

[2] Political violence by the drug cartels began in 1980, probably in response to treaties signed with the United States on extradition, in 1979, and on mutual legal assistance in narcotics matters, in 1981. The death squad, *Muerte a Secuestradores* or MAS, (Death to Kidnappers) was founded in 1981. A few days before the inauguration of President Belisario Betancur in 1982, the cartels attempted to assassinate Attorney General Gonzalez Charry, who had played a role in drafting both treaties. Politically motivated violence by the Medellín cartel grew exponentially in the Betancur and Barco years.

The "drug war" has also increased the killing and human suffering in Colombia. After provoking a military response by murdering Galán and other civilian leaders, the Medellín cartel responded to the pressure on its leaders with a murderous terrorist campaign of its own. It placed bombs in public places, including an aircraft in flight and the main offices of newspapers, and it killed innocent bystanders in attempting to assassinate top law-enforcement officers. The police units carrying out the war on drug trafficking also committed serious abuses: suspects "disappeared" after their arrest, many detainees were tortured, and in neighborhoods of Medellín the police arrested young people indiscriminately and at times opened fire in crowded public places.

The U.S. government has taken a great interest in the Colombian anti-trafficking efforts, and has supported the Army and police with training and unprecedented military aid. But while urging Army involvement in the fight against drug traffickers, the Bush administration has ignored the repressive practices of the Colombian military, which makes it ineligible for aid under the foreign-assistance laws of the United States. Colombian military leaders have openly announced that they will use the U.S. aid for their own counterinsurgency purposes, thus making clear that it will support the continuation of this "dirty war." Despite the "war on drugs," Colombian Army leaders continue their counterinsurgency efforts in unholy alliance with drug traffickers, through their joint sponsorship of paramilitary gangs.

The aggressive campaign to arrest and extradite drug traffickers is also increasingly clouded by human rights violations committed by specialized police units that enjoy generous aid from the United States. As a result, the Bush administration cannot escape responsibility for the serious violations of human rights that are being committed under the guise of a "war on drugs."

In the meantime, a decades-old insurgency war continues to disrupt the lives of many Colombians. Several guerrilla groups in different parts of the country continue to engage the Colombian armed forces in combat. Each guerilla group also regularly violates the laws of war: they kidnap civilians for ransom and they murder civilian authorities and political opponents. The Colombian Army, too, conducts its counterinsurgency war in violation of international humanitarian law. In addition to the crimes of Army-sponsored "self-defense groups" and the forcible recruitment of civilians into them, the Army has bombed and strafed rural areas without regard to the safety of noncombatants. Military and police forces have also been directly responsible for many cases of political murder, forced disappearance and torture of political opponents.

This report documents these patterns of abuse and provides some examples. It also describes several ways in which the Colombian government and other state institutions have responded to this human rights crisis, and provides an assessment of those efforts. Judges and prosecutors have made some courageous efforts to halt the violence and bring the perpetrators to justice, and they have suffered terrifying reprisals. So far, government protection of them has been inadequate.

Not surprisingly, there have been successful prosecutions of human rights violations in only three cases. In the case known as Altos del Portal, the Army had a great interest in punishing officers who had murdered prisoners while conducting an operation at the behest of a prominent drug trafficker. In the murder of Afranio Parra, a leader of the Movimiento 19 de Abril (M-19), the Barco administration wanted to punish the policemen who killed him to signal the government's good faith in pursuing peace negotiations with that guerrilla organization. In the case known as La Rochela, the paramilitary-group members who killed two judges and ten investigators in January 1989 have been severely punished, but their two supporters in the Army got off lightly, and one of them escaped under suspicious circumstances.

The Colombian government reached a peace agreement with the M-19 after protracted negotiations. The agreement has opened an important avenue for the political participation of sectors of Colombian society that have until now been disenfranchised. This initial success has led to encouraging first steps in peace talks with a larger organization, the Ejército Popular de Liberación (EPL), and two smaller groups. The two most active guerrilla groups, Ejército de Liberación Nacional (ELN) and the Fuerzas Armadas Revolucioharias de Colombia (FARC), continue their armed struggle as of this writing, even though the FARC has continued to express a willingness to engage in talks.

For several years, Colombia has been governed under a state of emergency that suspends many fundamental rights.[3] The state of emergency grants the President extraordinary powers which have been frequently used to suspend due process and to restrict freedom of

---

[3] President Turbay had lifted the state of siege in July 1982; President Betancur reimposed it on May 1, 1984, and it has been in effect throughout the nation ever since.

association. Despite increasingly vicious political strife, and the continued use of "dirty war" tactics by agents of the state, most Colombians may take part in a free and vigorous political debate and are able to join a variety of organizations of civil society. But the government's increasing exercise of its emergency powers has slowly eroded these fundamental freedoms. Although these powers have been used in some cases for the laudable purpose of curbing paramilitary violence, the cost has been to limit the enjoyment of some basic rights.

On August 7, 1990, César Gaviria Trujillo became the President of Colombia. The date marked the end of the four-year term of Virgilio Barco, during which the civilian authorities of Colombia attempted to fashion creative solutions to the country's political violence. Unfortunately, the transition finds Colombia still beset by terrible violence. Murder claims some 23,000 lives each year, one of the highest per capita murder rates in the world. Approximately 4,000 lives were lost in political violence in 1988 and 3,200 in 1989; these figures, as noted, are the highest in the hemisphere in those years. In the first few months of 1990, the situation worsened, possibly as a result of the political passions aroused by the presidential election. Politically motivated murders increased, and their victims included prominent leaders and two other presidential contenders, stunning a nation accustomed to political violence.

The cold statistical information would indicate that all efforts to counter the violence have failed miserably. We believe, however, that it is important to analyze those efforts in some depth to see why they have failed. We also have tremendous faith in Colombia's great reservoir of talent and human courage, which has offered constantly renewed hope that new ways may be found to solve the problem of political violence. President Gaviria is in a position, early in his term, to benefit from past experience and to breathe new life into peace-making efforts. That is why we believe it is important to review the current state of several initiatives taken in recent years in the course of the peace process with leftist insurgencies, the campaign to disarm and outlaw civil defense groups and the so-called "war on drug trafficking."

In previous reports, Americas Watch has chronicled the many tragic instances of human rights violations by all sides in the Colombian struggle, as well as the efforts of many brave Colombians, within and outside the civilian government and in different agencies and institutions, to bring these violations to an end. The present report attempts to take stock of those efforts at a time when a new administration has taken office. The administration enters with the undeniable advantage of a significant popular mandate obtained in elections that, despite violence against contenders, were widely accepted as free and fair. Mr. Gaviria belongs to the same party as Mr. Barco; in the latter's cabinet, he was successively Minister of the Treasury and of the Interior. Significantly, as Minister of Interior, Gaviria presented to the Colombian Congress a report listing 138 paramilitary groups identified by the government as responsible for executing "private justice." For those reasons, he might be expected to pursue Barco's anti-paramilitary policies. On the other hand, his electoral victory might encourage him to try new and different approaches.

In his first few weeks in office, Gaviria has announced policy objectives along the same lines as the previous administration, and he has called peace his "historic challenge." As discussed later in this report, he has also offered immunity from extradition and reduction of sentences to some suspected of involvement in drug trafficking and in paramilitary violence, in exchange for testimony against their former accomplices. He has created a new position as Presidential Counsellor on Security, in charge of coordinating police and security forces involved in drug interdiction and in the anti-paramilitary campaign, and has appointed Rafael Pardo to that position. Mr. Pardo distinguished himself as Barco's Counsellor for Peace. A close Pardo aide, Jesús Antonio Bejarano, has been named Counsellor for Peace. Gaviria also named Jorge Orlando Melo, a noted social scientist and researcher, as Counsellor for Human Rights. It appears, therefore, that in these areas there will be a strong element of continuity with Barco's plans.

We believe that this is an appropriate moment to reflect on the achievements and failures of the policies of the recent past. They offer important lessons not only for Colombians, but also for other Latin Americans who are faced with similar problems. These issues are already the subject of important and illuminating debate in Colombia. With this report, Americas Watch hopes to contribute to that debate from the perspective of an international human rights organization.

In our view, the continued violence does not mean that the policies of seeking peace and combatting paramilitary violence were wrong in theory. We do believe, however, that there were serious problems in their implementation and execution. More importantly, they failed because they avoided confronting the powers that stood in the way of successful investigations and prosecutions when the evidence led to high-ranking officers. The high command of the Army did not publicly object to these initiatives, but never cooperated with investigations and at times obstructed them. The civilian government led a forceful campaign against hired assassins and private parties engaged in paramilitary violence, but it evaded acknowledging that these private parties acted with the support and encouragement of agents of the armed and security forces.

In the following pages we provide more detailed information about the implementation of these measures, and about their disappointing results. That information highlights the lack of resolve on the part of civilian authorities in pursuing cases when there was evidence of complicity by military or police officers. In our view, that has been the main reason why some promising steps yielded such discouraging results. The links between military authorities and paramilitary violence must be probed by the Gaviria administration if it is to make further headway than its predecessor in curbing political killings in Colombia.

II. Paramilitary Violence

Paramilitary activity in Colombia has become the most important element of political violence in the country, a situation which has not changed since our last report. The Colombian government has recognized the frightening incidence of paramilitary violence, as well as the devastating implications of "private justice" on both the security of its citizens and the relevance and legitimacy of the state. The government should be commended for the steps it has taken to combat such activity, but further measures must still be implemented to rectify the deficiencies of its chosen strategies. In particular, the government must make a greater effort to pursue investigations into instances of paramilitary violence in which members of government forces are implicated. In addition, the government must take steps to guarantee the safety of justice officials—judges, prosecutors, investigators—and of witnesses, so that those responsible for paramilitary violence may be identified, prosecuted and punished.

A. The Distinction Between Self-defense Groups and Paramilitary Groups

"Private justice" in Colombia is carried out by self-defense groups, paramilitary groups and hired assassins known as *sicarios*. Self-defense groups were initially created by certain landowners in conjunction with the Army, ostensibly to protect property and individuals from guerrilla forces. They were most prevalent in areas where the rebel presence was strong and the influence of government forces limited. Provided with weapons by the Armed Forces—as authorized by Decree 3398 of 1965 and Law 48 of 1968, discussed below—self-defense groups were intended to complement official counterinsurgency efforts.

Paramilitary groups are offensive units designed to identify and eliminate political opponents perceived as posing a threat to established interests. Organized by large landowners and, more recently, by major drug traffickers, they operate as their sponsors' private armies. Despite official declarations to the contrary, these groups are "paramilitary" in nature because they act with the complicity of government forces which, at the very least, look the other way or, at worst, directly participate in their violence. Their targets include labor organizers, teachers, journalists, human rights monitors and leftist politicians, particularly members of the Unión Patriótica (UP). Drug traffickers have frequently become large landowners and in the process have come to share the right-wing politics of many traditional landowners, and as such they have assumed the leadership of some of the most notorious paramilitary groups.

Sicarios are roaming, hired assassins, who have been trained in well-financed schools supplied with sophisticated weapons. They often operate in mobile paramilitary hit squads. Generally viewed as a product of the lucrative drug trade, hired killers in fact have a history in Colombia, dating at least from the period of "La Violencia."[4] Known then as *pájaros*, the killers were contracted then by landowners and political bosses.[5]

There is a certain artificiality, however, to the distinctions drawn here among self-defense groups, paramilitary groups and *sicarios*, since their actions overlap to a large extent. Over time, many self-defense groups have moved beyond defense to take on the targeted assassination of actual or perceived opponents, becoming, in effect, paramilitary groups. Paramilitary groups, meanwhile, have often claimed to be self-defense groups, in an attempt to appropriate the latter's state-endowed legitimacy. Such claims may also reflect the origins of some of the most notorious paramilitary groups. *Sicarios* are often members of paramilitary or self-defense groups, even if they frequently seem to act alone. The use of hired guns for particularly significant political murders is a tactic designed to sow confusion over the identity of the "intellectual

---

[4] "La Violencia" is the period between 1948 and 1953, in which rival political factions waged civil war in Colombia.

[5] North American Congress on Latin America (NACLA), *Report on the Americas*, "Colombia Cracks Up," Volume XXIII, Number 6, April 1990, p. 14

authors" of the crime. In the same spirit, minors are often hired as *sicarios* so that, if caught, they will not be tried by criminal courts but placed under the protection of the jurisdiction for minors.

The range of actors engaged in political violence today makes it impossible to determine with any certainty which groups belong to which category. To our knowledge, no one has kept track of the number of self-defense groups created by the Army in the 25-year history of this strategy. Similarly, it is hard to say whether a group that claims self-defense status was actually created under the authority of Law 48. If paramilitary and self-defense groups are theoretically distinguishable in origin, they have become virtually indistinguishable in the way they operate, both intimidating and murdering civilians whom they identify as supporters of leftist causes.

B. The Legal History; Interpretations

In 1968, the Congress of Colombia adopted Law 48 without much parliamentary debate. It incorporated the text of Legislative Decree 3398, which had been issued in 1965. The law allowed the government to "mobilize the population in activities and tasks" to restore normalcy. In addition, the new law read, in part:

> The Ministry of National Defense, through the authorized commanders, may provide, when deemed appropriate, as personal property, weapons that are considered the exclusive use of the Armed Forces.[6]

The legislation allowed for the formation of what came to be known as self-defense groups, essentially groups of private citizens armed by the government to defend themselves from leftist guerrillas. Over time, however, many of the groups became private offensive armies, financed

---

[6] Consejería Presidencial para la Defensa, Protección y Promoción de los Derechos Humanos, *Boletín Informativo*, Bogotá, D.E.: Imprenta Nacional de Colombia, Marzo-Abril 1989, p. 12.

by wealthy landowners or drug traffickers to terrorize and kill civilian leftist opponents.

Even as violence by private armies grew, high-ranking Army officers refused to declare that self-defense groups were illegal. Civilian authorities tried to explain that under Law 48, only the President was allowed to create and form self-defense groups, so that associations claiming to be self-defense had no legal standing unless a presidential decree had established them. Many of these groups had been in operation for years; unfortunately, the civilian leaders made no attempt to identify which groups had or had not been properly created. In addition, it was apparent that military leaders did not necessarily agree with such a benign interpretation: a Ministry of Defense memorandum of 1987 told Army subordinates that ". . . organizing, training and supporting self-defense groups must be a permanent objective of the military force, where [those groups] are loyal and manifest themselves against the enemy."[7] As late as November 1988, Defense Minister Gen. Rafael Samudio insisted on the legitimacy of self-defense groups. In fact, some civilian cabinet members seemed in 1987 to agree with Samudio. Minister of Justice José Manuel Arias Carrizosa sided with him in a parliamentary debate on the topic; significantly, César Gaviria, who was then also a Cabinet member, publicly dissented.[8]

Only after Samudio was replaced by Gen. Manuel Jaime Guerrero Paz in late 1988 did the Army change its official position on this matter. Soon after assuming his post, Guerrero Paz was quoted in *Semana* magazine as saying, "Any organization of subversive or terrorist type, or of *sicarios* or paramilitary and [sic] of private justice, must be relentlessly persecuted."[9] The phrase, of course, left open the possibility that legally-constituted self-defense groups would continue to exist; it was

---

[7] *Semana*, May 2, 1988, p. 35.

[8] Americas Watch, *The Killings in Colombia* (New York: Americas Watch Committee, April 1989), pp. 50-51. Ultimately, advocates for banning self-defense groups carried the day; Samudio and Arias Carrizosa were removed. It appears, however, that as a *quid pro quo* those who prevailed had to concede on the enactment of the Statute for the Defense of Democracy.

[9] Ibid., p. 51.

important, however, that the Army's highest-ranking officer for the first time condemned paramilitary and private justice groups by name. As stated elsewhere in this report, the change in the Army may be in words alone. Guerrero Paz did support the government on the peace process, but apparently moved slowly in confronting the paramilitary phenomenon. His replacement as Minister of Defense, General Oscar Botero, is said to have gradually moved the Army in the direction of accepting the official anti-paramilitary line. Gaviria has confirmed Botero as his Minister of Defense.

In April 1989, the Colombian government issued three decrees aimed at curbing paramilitary violence.[10] The first, Decree 813, called for the formation of a commission responsible for advising the government and coordinating a range of anti-paramilitary efforts. The commission is comprised of the Ministers of Government, Justice and National Defense as well as the chiefs of the government security forces, including the Army, the National Police and the Departamento Administrativo de Seguridad (DAS).[11] Its mission is to draw up plans to curb paramilitary violence, coordinate implementation of its proposals and evaluate the effectiveness of these measures. The decree mandates the cooperation of all security forces, on pain of punishment.

Decree 814 established a 1000-member special force, comprised of selected active-duty National Police officers, to "carry out missions of public order" against paramilitary groups. The special force is under the direction of the Chief of the National Police, with the support of the commission created by Decree 813. The force is to function so long as the country remains under a state of siege.

The third decree, Decree 815, is perhaps the most significant. It suspends the Armed Forces' authority—established over 20 years earlier under Law 48—to distribute weapons to civilians. It also requires self-defense groups to be authorized not only by presidential decree, but also by the Ministers of Defense and Government, thereby clarifying the

---

[10] *News From Americas Watch*, "Colombian Government Adopts Measures to Combat Paramilitary Death Squads," Number 5, July 1989.

[11] DAS is a uniformed investigative and intelligence-gathering body under the authority of the President.

authority to create self-defense groups. Moreover, the decree explicitly limits these groups to defensive actions—such as guarding premises—and bars their participation in combat. In May 1989, the Colombian Supreme Court declared unconstitutional the Army's authorization to distribute weapons to civilians, thus turning the "suspension" dictated by Decree 815 into a permanent prohibition. While this decision comes 25 years too late, it is now illegal in Colombian law for the Army to give weapons to civilians.[12]

The thrust of Decree 815 was to put an end to the Armed Forces' unilateral creation of self-defense groups and, by extension, the paramilitary bands into which they evolved. The government did not, however, outlaw existing groups by name nor did it declare that existing authorized groups must be reauthorized under the new, more stringent standards. As a result, self-defense groups formed legally under Law 48 might be able to claim legal existence. In fact, the decree allows the Army to continue using this questionable tactic, provided the proper signatures (President, Minister of Defense and Minister of Government) are obtained, albeit with limitations as to the distribution of weapons and engagement in offensive operations. There remains, therefore, some confusion as to what Army officers can do with regards to self-defense groups.

In June 1989, the Barco administration attempted to correct these deficiencies by issuing Decree 1194, which established criminal penalties for civilians and members of the Armed Forces who recruit, train, promote, finance, organize, lead or belong to the "armed groups, misnamed paramilitary groups, which have been formed into death squads, bands of hired assassins, self-defense groups, or groups that carry out their own justice." Significantly, when those convicted are active or retired members of any official security force prison sentences are to be increased by one-third to one-half.

These efforts have put many paramilitary groups in a defensive posture in the past year. Retreating from the arrogance of prior years, spokesmen have publicly attempted to cast them as self-defense organizations in an effort to claim the legitimacy that previously

---

[12] Comisión Andina de Juristas, Sección Colombiana, *Informativo Legislativo y Jurisprudencial*, Abril-Mayo-Junio 1989, p. 67a.

authorized self-defense groups continue to enjoy. In one particularly bizarre example of this, Luis Ramírez, leader of a paramilitary association, adamantly told a reporter that his was a legitimate self-defense group:

> We have fallen into the trap that the communist left has wanted us to fall into. They are calling 'paramilitaries' those brave, civilian peasants who have wanted to rout the guerrillas. But since we do not have the weapons or possess the uniforms that are of the exclusive use of the Armed Forces, we are not 'paramilitaries.' We are born peasants.[13]

A week later it was reported that Ramírez was actually León Guillermo Tarazona, a former army captain who was discharged in November 1988 for bad behavior.[14]

In spite of the pressure felt by some paramilitary groups, the decrees have not significantly reduced paramilitary violence. The main reason for this is the government's failure to seriously investigate allegations of official involvement in the paramilitary sphere. In some cases, massacres and targeted killings have taken place in areas under strict military control, prompting the question why the assassins had such extraordinary freedom of movement (see, for example, the discussion of the Pueblo Bello massacre below). Several prominent UP members have been assassinated shortly after they were denied continued official protection or on days when their bodyguards simply failed to show up. Americas Watch said last year that "the Barco administration took some brave steps in 1989, first to outlaw the 'paramilitary groups,' and then to prosecute some of their junior members. But it has yet to conduct aggressive inquiries into the connections between these groups and high-

---

[13] "'No somos paramilitares,' dice jefe de autodefensas," *El Tiempo*, 21 June 1989.

[14] "El jefe de autodefensas es un ex capitán del Ejército," *El Tiempo*, June 28, 1989.

ranking military officers."[15] That assessment remained unchanged in the Barco administration's last year and still stands as Gaviria enters his third month in office.

Another reason for the partial failure of the Barco policy against paramilitary violence is the judiciary's continuing inability to keep up with the escalating number of vicious crimes that need to be investigated and prosecuted. Despite governmental pledges to strengthen and support the criminal justice system, the judiciary continues to be hampered by insufficient funding, inadequate protection and, at crucial moments, a lack of cooperation with its investigations. Some of the blame lies with certain members of the judiciary who maintain a "business as usual" attitude, conducting lackluster investigations and hiding behind technicalities and bureaucratic obstacles, and occasionally allowing themselves to be corrupted or intimidated. But many judges, prosecutors and court officials have performed their jobs seriously and conscientiously. These brave public servants have all too often been stymied by inadequate government support and protection.[16]

Americas Watch calls on the Gaviria administration to ensure that investigations of suspected links between paramilitary and government forces are initiated and pursued. We also believe that the Colombian government should unequivocally renounce the strategy of civil defense and remove all traces of legality from existing groups. Communities that decide to defend their lives and property with their own guns should be regulated carefully so that they engage in strictly defensive actions and individual participation in those actions is strictly voluntary. For the new legislation to reap significant change, members of official forces who are facilitating or participating in the work of paramilitary groups must be identified, removed from their posts, prosecuted and punished.

---

[15] Human Rights Watch, *The Bush Administration's Record on Human Rights in 1989* (New York: Human Rights Watch, January 1990), p. 65.

[16] The government has made some effort to protect judges, mostly by cloaking their identity and work in secrecy. We discuss these measures, and their effect, in Chapter VI.

C. The Role of the Army in Promoting Self-defense Groups

From the promulgation of Legislative Decree 3398 in 1965 until the issuance of Decree 815 in 1989, the Colombian Army played an extensive and public role in the creation and promotion of self-defense groups. Reflecting on this period, Defense Minister General Oscar Botero Restrepo explained that the Armed Forces "organized the peasant self-defense groups with eminently defensive criteria [and they] fulfilled their purpose throughout most of the national territory."[17] He also argued that the groups were effective until drug trafficking and unspecified other factors induced them to work on behalf of "perverse interests."[18]

Since the April 1989 decrees, the Army has sought to distance itself from the self-defense groups. According to General Botero, the Elite Force created by Decree 814 was organized:

> . . . to combat the groups of *sicarios* and the self-defense groups were dismantled. As a result, some of the ones that survive today are nothing more than bands of common criminals at the service of the drug traffic and private interests.[19]

It is good for the Army to take such a clear public position, but the facts on the ground are not necessarily that clear. While Americas Watch has no information that the Armed Forces continue to provide weapons to civilians, their association with the self-defense groups has never been limited to just that. There is strong evidence of continued official collaboration with those self-defense groups that conduct offensive operations, especially a frequent practice of "looking the other way." (See description below of the Pueblo Bello massacre and update on the Segovia massacre.) There is also evidence that Army officers continue to

---

[17] "Una calumnia a las Fuerzas Armadas," *El Tiempo*, March 30, 1990.

[18] Ibid.

[19] Ibid.

promote self-defense groups, often by force, in spite of the 1989 decrees (see Chapter IV).

Whether the Army's continued involvement with self-defense groups is the result of extensive—though perhaps not systemic—complicity with drug traffickers and other powerful interests, or originates in the highest levels of the Colombian armed forces, is a source of debate. Regardless, the government's new strategy of outlawing and disarming self-defense groups is not working because the Army has ignored it and refused to cooperate. Furthermore, claiming that such groups now lie outside state control has allowed the government to shirk the responsibility of keeping its house clean, and to falsely deny state participation in wide scale human rights abuse. Mr. Gaviria must acknowledge that well-placed officers in the Armed Forces continue to play the self-defense and paramilitary card, and take appropriate steps to sever this connection.

D. The Roles of the Medellín Cartel and of Landowners

Initially as a by-product of their illicit business, both the Medellín and Cali cocaine cartels have played significant roles in organizing, training, arming and maintaining armed death squads. Large landowners and businessmen (such as emerald miners) have also formed private armies to defend their interests by violent means. As their wealth accumulated over time, the drug traffickers sought to complement their economic status with social acceptance. They purchased vast tracts of land from farmers who, because of the leftist insurgency, were willing to sell cheaply, and they invested heavily in legitimate business ventures such as urban construction and banks. They became the benefactors of their cities, making infrastructure improvements which the government was unable to provide, and gaining a certain degree of popular support locally.

As landowners in conflictive regions, the traffickers came in contact with other large landowners who had created self-defense groups to counter rebel kidnappings, extortion and war taxes. Trafficking profits enabled Medellín chiefs Pablo Escobar and Gonzalo Rodríguez Gacha[20] to contribute to these efforts by developing *escuelas de sicarios,* well funded and equipped schools to train assassins. Several schools have been discovered in the Magdalena Medio region, producing some of the most efficient assassins in Colombia, many of whom have joined paramilitary groups. As explained elsewhere in this report, training in some of these schools was provided by Israeli and British mercenaries who had had contacts with their nations' intelligence services.

Given their new economic interests, the drug traffickers have also come to share the reactionary views of local landowners. Consequently, their paramilitary groups have targeted advocates of economic and social change. Through targeted assassinations, they have cleared portions of the Magdalena Medio region of virtually all opposition activity—civilian or armed—establishing, in one town, what the North American Congress on Latin America (NACLA) termed "a kind of independent paramilitary republic."[21] In addition, as the cartels diversify their investments, the lines separating traffickers from cattlemen and emerald miners have also blurred. To some extent, their private gangs have tended to merge and have increasingly engaged in killings of a political nature.

In a practice referred to as *limpieza social* (social cleansing), paramilitary groups have also carried out killings of homosexuals, beggars, the mentally ill, prostitutes and drug addicts. These killings have been most common in Antioquia and Valle del Cauca provinces, particularly in Medellín and Cali. Some 66 such killings were reported in the first quarter of 1990 alone.[22] There is an apparent degree of local popular support for, or at least apathy toward, this "cleaning up of the neighborhood." Though paramilitary groups using a variety of names often claim credit for these crimes, the available evidence suggests that the murders are committed by off-duty police. Though the matter is

---

[20] Gonzalo Rodríguez Gacha was killed in a shoot-out with police in December 1989.

[21] NACLA, "Colombia Cracks Up," p. 27.

[22] Comisión Intercongregacional de Justicia y Paz, *Justicia y Paz,* Vol. 3, No. 1, January-March 1990.

debatable, this would be an instance in which paramilitary groups are not financed or supported by the cartels. Americas Watch has received no information indicating that authorities have even said they would investigate these killings.

The Colombian government has consistently blamed all paramilitary violence on the drug cartels, primarily on the Medellín group headed by Pablo Escobar. There is a large element of truth to these assertions, but they are also a convenient way of ignoring the role of other forces, including agents of the state. The Medellín cartel has penetrated many institutions of Colombian society, and enjoys assistance from many quarters. An embarrassing example is the Altos del Portal case discussed in Chapter VI. The United States government, for its part, has insisted on linking Escobar and his cronies with left-wing terrorism. Here, again, there is an element of truth. The FARC collects "war taxes" from all citizens, regardless of their source of income; in some areas, this means that the FARC extorts money from drug dealers. Rebels impose minimum prices for coca leaves, a practice which supports small-scale growers who are seen by the FARC as potential supporters. There have also been sporadic reports of arms deals between traffickers and rebels. As we discussed in our April 1989 report, however, this collaboration pales next to the bloody targeting by the cartel-supported paramilitary groups of leftist politicians and peasant communities that are considered the "social base" of the guerrillas.[23]

The cartels have also received some international assistance. In May 1990, it was discovered that hundreds of weapons found on a ranch owned by the late Rodríguez Gacha had been sold by an Israeli arms manufacturer in March 1989 to the government of Antigua. Antigua has denied ever ordering or receiving the weapons, while Israel continues to accuse it of violating the "end user" assurances contained in the purchasing agreement.

---

[23] Virgilio Barco himself has cast doubt on the existence of a "narco-guerrilla," so often denounced by United States officials: "The term 'narco-guerrilla' which implies a permanent alliance is misleading." Quoted in Paul H. Bocker, *Lost Illusions: Latin America's Struggle for Democracy as Recounted by its Leaders* (New York: Markus Wiener, 1990), p. 200.

Two Israelis, Yair Klein and Maurice Sarfati, have been accused of transferring the weapons.[24]   Klein, who owns a private security company, says he has no idea how the weapons got into Rodríguez Gacha's hands. He says he was in Antigua to provide military training to Panamanian exiles seeking to overthrow then-Panamanian leader Manuel Antonio Noriega.[25] The project was abandoned before the United States invasion of Panama, when the weapons were still at sea. According to Klein, the weapons were then supposed to be delivered to Panama but "somehow ended up" in Colombia.

Sarfati, the owner of a heavily indebted agricultural products company in Antigua, reportedly served as the contact person between the Israeli and Antiguan governments.   An investigation conducted by Antigua found that the weapons had been diverted to Colombia after being loaded to another ship in an Antiguan port. It also determined that the role of Antigua had been only to provide fake "user certificates" for the sale of Israeli weapons. The operation was directed by Klein and Sarfati and financed by Bank Hapoalim, an Israeli bank.

Colombian newspapers reported that the weapons entered Colombia at the port of San Antero, in northern Córdoba. Villagers there contend that the weapons were taken in a truck to nearby San Andrés de Sotavento, where Rodríguez Gacha and Fidel Castaño, a wealthy rancher, flew the weapons to some point in Cundinamarca. The

---

[24] In 1989, Klein was accused of training paramilitary groups for the Medellín cartel, but he denied the charge, claiming instead to be teaching self-defense to farmers. However, videotapes that Klein has produced to promote his business show notorious members of Magdalena Medio paramilitary groups. One of them has been convicted of the murder of judges and court officials in La Rochela in 1989. According to a DAS report, in late 1987, Klein and his team left Colombia and went to Honduras for the purpose of providing training for United States-supported Nicaraguan *contras*.

[25] Klein was working with Colonel Eduardo Herrera Hassan, who was then living in Miami after a failed CIA-sponsored coup against Noriega. Until August 1990, Herrera Hassan was the top law-enforcement official in the post-invasion Panamanian government.

reports noted that, despite widespread knowledge of this transaction, no authority bothered to investigate it.[26]

Paramilitary activity has also been promoted by wealthy landowners, especially in the Magdalena Medio and Urabá regions. Fidel Castaño, in particular, has emerged in the past few years as a prominent force behind much of the paramilitary violence in the Urabá region. Castaño, who likes to be known as "Rambo," owns two ranches in Córdoba—Las Tangas and Jaraguay—which he reportedly purchased with money made trafficking in drugs. He is a rabid anti-Communist, apparently the result of the 1984 abduction and murder of his father by the FARC. In April, Rogelio de Jesús Escobar Mejía, one of Castaño's *sicarios*, deserted and turned himself in to DAS. The information provided by Escobar Mejía led DAS to several mass graves on Castaño's properties, containing some 26 bodies, including at least seven identified as peasants who had been abducted in the Pueblo Bello incident (see below). With the discovery of other graves the body count could reach 100.[27]

According to government reports, Castaño has close ties with Pablo Escobar and is assuming the military leadership of the Medellín cartel, the role held by Rodríguez Gacha before his death. A U.S. official told the *Washington Post* in May, "Fidel Castaño is the enforcer for the cartel. He provides the muscle."[28] Escobar Mejía told investigators that Castaño runs a paramilitary operation of 120 members and that in the 16 months he was part of the group, it executed 95 people. The philosophy behind Castaño's violence is to rid the region not only of leftist guerrillas, but also of collaborators and "collaborators of collaborators." He has been linked to several massacres in addition to Pueblo Bello, including the 1988 killings of peasants in the town of La

---

[26] This account was drawn from "Armas a Antigua despachadas junto a cohetes para Colombia," *El Espectador*, May 10, 1990; "Más países habrían pasado armas para 'El Mexicano'," *El Tiempo*, May 10, 1990; "'Guerra' de explicaciones por las armas," *El Espectador*, May 9, 1990; and "Israeli Arms, Ticketed to Antigua, Now in a Colombia Drug Arsenal," *New York Times*, May 6, 1990.

[27] "Cartel Enforcer Linked to Massacres," *Washington Post*, May 6, 1990.

[28] Ibid.

Mejor Esquina and banana workers from two plantations in Urabá, La Negra and La Honduras.[29]

Of greatest concern to Americas Watch is the apparent link between Castaño and government forces in the zone. According to one press account, a confidential DAS document reveals "a compromising link between multiple officials of the public force and Fidel Castaño."[30] In apparent recognition of this link, the National Police Elite Force was sent instead of local authorities to conduct the investigation that led to the discovery of the mass graves and to exhume the bodies.[31] Castaño has not been apprehended; some observers believe he may have fled Colombia.

Another well-known leader of the paramilitary groups, Henry Pérez, remains at large, though his responsibility for many killings has been known for years. Pérez is the leader of ACDEGAM, the Peasant Association of Cattlemen and Farmers of the Magdalena Medio, which is perhaps the most notorious of the civil-defense-turned-paramilitary groups. According to Colombian authorities, he was an Army-trained civil defense leader before joining forces with the drug cartel. Pérez still exerts formidable political power in the area of Puerto Boyacá, the heart of the Magdalena Medio region, and has managed to avoid arrest on dozens of serious charges while sending messages to the press from supposed "hiding places."[32]

On May 11, 1990, Iván Roberto Duque, representing 15 self-defense groups in Magdalena Medio with some 4,000 members, met with Minister of Government Horacio Serpa Uribe. Duque, a congressional deputy, delivered a document in which the groups "manifest[ed] their desire to lay down their weapons and demobilize, in exchange for the government's establishing an effective presence, military as well as social,

---

[29] For more detailed discussion of these incidents, see Americas Watch, *The Killings in Colombia*.

[30] "Rambo," *Semana*, April 24, 1990.

[31] Ibid.

[32] Ana Arana, "Colombia now hunts former top drug enforcer," *Miami Herald*, September 16, 1990.

in Magdalena Medio." According to press reports, the groups' decision to enter into negotiations with the government was the product not only of the April 1989 decrees but also of accusations linking self-defense groups with paramilitary groups and drug trafficking and of the belief that the Elite Force had turned the Magdalena Medio into a center of operations against the Medellín cartel.[33]   The government's initial response to the offer of negotiations was cool. Minister Serpa said that no conversations could take place until the paramilitary groups laid down their arms.   This also seems to be the stance of the Gaviria administration, which has continued discussions with leftist insurgencies such as the EPL, Quintín Lame and Partido Revolucionario de los Trabajadores (PRT), but so far refuses to agree to Duque's offer. Instead, Gaviria has made an alternative offer. On September 5, 1990, he issued a decree giving lower and middle-level drug traffickers the opportunity to turn themselves in and be tried in Colombian courts, return criminal proceeds, confess, and provide intelligence information. In exchange, they are offered immunity from extradition and reduced sentences.   The measure also applies to members of paramilitary groups. But a few days later paramilitary leader Henry Pérez stated that he would reject the offer, even while denying links to drug trafficking.[34]

E. The Growth of Paramilitary Violence in 1988 and 1989

Deaths from paramilitary violence totalled in the thousands in 1988 and 1989. In 1988, paramilitary groups with clear ties to Escobar and Rodríguez Gacha were responsible for the largest number of politically motivated crimes, as well as for massacres in places like Urabá and Segovia.   In 1989, the proportion of cases attributable to cartel-financed groups declined (a detailed discussion of the relevant statistics

---

[33] "Las autodefensas quieren desarmarse," *El Tiempo*, May 11, 1990.

[34] Ana Arana, "Colombia changes course in drug war strategy," *Miami Herald*, September 7, 1990; Douglas Farah, "Colombia Offers Drug Lords a Deal," *Washington Post*, September 7, 1990; Arana, "Colombia now hunts...," *Miami Herald*.

is presented in Chapter V). The decline may be the product of the government's campaign against paramilitary violence, although more likely it is due to its active pursuit of the leadership of the Medellín cartel in the course of the "war on drugs" declared in August 1989. As detailed later in this chapter, however, the "war" has not stopped paramilitary violence, which even increased in early 1990. A possible explanation is that paramilitary groups have been able to continue operating because they were never really dependent on cartel money; instead, they have simply reverted to traditional sources of funding from landowners, emerald traders and other powerful interests, coupled with local support of Army officers.

Barrancabermeja is the latest staging ground for political violence in Colombia. Earlier this year, in a special report on Colombia, NACLA observed:

> During 1988 the paramilitary groups extended their control over much of Magdalena Medio, successfully driving the guerrillas from what had been a major stronghold. . . . Puerto Boyacá has become a kind of independent paramilitary republic. . . . The Right then laid siege to Barrancabermeja, the center of Left activity. Two hundred popular leaders and activists were killed in 1988."[35]

In May, Americas Watch visited Barrancabermeja and obtained testimony from local human rights groups. The city is in the center of the Magdalena Medio region and is home to some 200,000 people. In the last three years, the region has witnessed some 650 politically motivated murders, a huge number for a city its size.

Several paramilitary groups operate in the region, most prominently the Colonel Correa Campos Command and MAS. The local human rights group, the Regional Committee for the Defense of Human Rights, contends that paramilitary activity is part of a government counterinsurgency strategy adopted after strictly military action and attempts at negotiation failed. "These bands of civilians are protected,

---

[35] See NACLA, "Colombia Cracks Up."

through action or omission, by the Military Forces, and they are advised technically and ideologically by the military bases seated in the zone," the Committee contends.[36]   Testimony obtained by Americas Watch in Barrancabermeja is discussed at greater length in Chapter IV.

F. Paramilitary Violence in 1990

The surge of paramilitary violence has continued unabated in 1990, and the targets remain unchanged.   One of the most infamous instances was the Pueblo Bello massacre, which occurred in the portion of the Urabá region that lies in Antioquia department. On January 13, as many as 42 peasants were abducted by a 52-man paramilitary squad.   The abduction was said to have been ordered by Fidel Castaño, who was searching for the killer of one of his associates and some cattle rustlers. He met with the squad at the Santa Mónica ranch and reportedly told the men, "Pueblo Bello is a nest of guerrillas and about 15 or 20 people must be picked up from there, hopefully alive."   The men were divided into four groups, each with a list of names.   The squad took the 42 men to one of Castaño's ranches, where they were tortured and killed.   As noted, details of the massacre were provided to investigators by Rodrigo de Jesús Escobar Mejía, a deserter, and some of the bodies found in the mass graves he revealed at Castaño's Las Tangas and Jaraguay ranches have been identified as those abducted from Pueblo Bello.[37]   Three men traveling in two vehicles in the region on the night of the massacre also disappeared.[38]

An especially troublesome aspect of the case is that the two trucks, carrying 42 prisoners and perhaps 30 armed men, passed unhindered through the roads of a heavily militarized zone.   The Delegate Prosecutor for Human Rights initiated disciplinary proceedings

---

[36] Comité Regional Para la Defensa de los Derechos Humanos, *Violaciones de los Derechos Humanos en la Región*, Barrancabermeja, Santander, April 1990.

[37] *"Rambo," Semana*, April 24, 1990.

[38] Comisión Intercongregacional de Justicia y Paz, *Justicia y Paz*.

against Captain Alvaro Gómez Duque and Sublieutenant Néstor Manrique Sierra, of the Voltígeros Battalion based in Urabá. These officers, who are charged with negligence for allowing passage of the trucks, were in charge of a roadblock at the entrance to Pueblo Bello, manned by 12 soldiers, on the night of the kidnappings. Disciplinary proceedings may result in their dishonorable discharge, without prejudice to criminal proceedings if warranted. To date, they have not been charged in the criminal investigation of the Pueblo Bello massacre.[39]

While the investigation into the massacre has proceeded, aided by the testimony of deserter Escobar Mejía, it has not led to the arrest of any of those who took part in the abduction and killings. Castaño is a shadowy figure who reportedly spends a good portion of his time in Paris, where he keeps a home, and New York. In a distressing setback, the state prosecutor investigating the case, María Ester Restrepo, was shot and killed together with her police bodyguard as they entered her office in Apartadó on July 24.[40]

Other instances of paramilitary violence in the first semester of 1990 include the following:

> February 26—Apartadó, Antioquia—UP Mayor Diana Stella Cardona was assassinated by five men who identified themselves as members of DAS.[41]

> February 26—Cimitarra, Santander—Journalist Silvia Margarita Duzán Sáenz and three men were killed in a café moments after her arrival in town. The three men—Josué Vargas Mateus, Saúl Castañeda and Miguel Angel Barajas—were leaders of the

---

[39] Douglas Farah, "Cartel Enforcer Linked to Massacres," *Washington Post*, May 6, 1990; *El Tiempo*, May 4, 1990; *La Prensa*, May 4, 1990; interview by Americas Watch with Procurator-Delegate for Human Rights Jaime Córdoba, Bogotá, May 1990.

[40] "State prosecutor killed by gunmen," *Miami Herald*, July 25, 1990.

[41] Ibid.

Association of Peasant Workers of Carare-Opón.[42]   A criminal investigation is pending before the 81st Court in Cimitarra, and an administrative inquiry by the Office of Special Investigations of the Procuraduría General de la Nación is also under way, examining the possible involvement of government agents. Neither inquiry has yielded findings, and no defendant has been identified. The two assassins are generally presumed to belong to paramilitary groups, but neither was known to the eyewitnesses to the attack.

March 1—Mocoa, Putumayo—Carmen Elisa Rosas Rosas, a judge, was assassinated along with three police agents on her way to town to take up her post. Officials claim the four were killed by the ELN, but others say she had received death threats from paramilitary groups linked to drug traffickers.[43]

March 13—Bogotá, D.E.—Tarcisio Roldán Palacios and his wife were killed in their apartment. Roldán was a former judge who was representing relatives of victims of the Segovia massacre.[44]

March 18—Apartadó, Antioquia—Six UP members were massacred in an ice cream parlor. A group of masked men forced them to lie on the ground and then shot them. Five others were hurt.[45]

March 27—Apartadó, Antioquia—A grenade thrown at a house while a judicial commission was there investigating the March 18 ice cream parlor killings. One person was killed in the attack

---

[42] "Asesinados la periodista Silvia Duzán y 3 dirigentes cívicos," *El Espectador,* February 27, 1990.

[43] Comisión Intercongregacional de Justicia y Paz, *Justicia y Paz.*

[44] Ibid.

[45] Ibid.

and seven were injured, including three court officials and a ten-year-old boy. The house was across the street from a police station, and though the attack took place at 6.35 p.m., the attackers left the scene unhindered.[46]

March 28—Chigorodó, Urabá region—Five leftists (two members of the UP and three of the Popular Front) were killed on two ranches.[47]

May 7—Pereira, Risaralda—A car bomb exploded in front of a building housing the Registraduría Municipal (Electoral Registry). One person was killed and five were wounded. Authorities blamed the Medellín cartel.[48]

May 8—Apartadó, Antioquia—The bodies of three UP members were found in a playground.[49]

G. Conclusions

While Americas Watch is concerned about all instances of human rights abuse in Colombia, we view paramilitary violence as especially worrisome. It not only violates the human rights of its victims but also contributes to a generalized sense of lawlessness, a threat which the state cannot endure.

With this in mind, Americas Watch reiterates its call to the Colombian government to give serious consideration to a strategy of disarming the civilian population. Private security agencies alone account

---

[46] *"Urabá: nuevos golpes contra Unión Patriótica,"* El Tiempo, March 29, 1990.

[47] Ibid.

[48] "El cartel detonó el primer carro/bomba en la región cafetera," *El Espectador,* May 9, 1990.

[49] "Asesinan a 3 miembros de UP en Urabá," *El Tiempo,* May 8, 1990.

for 50,000 armed men, which is almost the same as the total number of police troops. This and other forms of private defense provide a veneer of legality to the possession of weapons and to the conduct of security operations by many individuals who are effectively outside official control. A careful but sweeping review of all gun permits, with stern penalties for those who refuse to give up their weapons, might be a fresh start in the right direction.

We also urge the Colombian government to initiate and pursue investigations into incidents of paramilitary violence and to prosecute and punish those responsible. It is of special importance to make those members of government forces involved in paramilitary violence aware, by both words and deeds, that such activity will no longer be treated with impunity. Equally important is the government's obligation to protect those involved in investigating and prosecuting violent offenders, including judges, prosecutors and witnesses.

III. The "War" Against Drug Trafficking

The dramatic shift in policy represented by the Barco government's declared "war" on drug trafficking has had inevitable repercussions for human rights. As explained in *The Killings in Colombia*, the Medellín cartel has long involved itself in political violence, in addition to the ordinary criminal violence that accompanies drug trafficking. The most frequent targets of its political violence have been members and leaders of the Unión Patriótica, peasant communities perceived as sympathetic to leftist guerrillas, and leaders and members of a variety of grass-roots organizations. The cartel has also for years ordered and financed the murder of high public officials who tried to enforce anti-trafficking laws, including prosecutors and judges.[50]

The threat of murder gradually also extended to politicians in the mainstream parties who spoke out against tolerance for the cartels' activities and who advocated tough anti-trafficking measures. By 1989, the drug lords had issued explicit threats to some public figures who favored extradition of suspected drug traffickers to the United States. Significantly, the name adopted by the clandestine unit behind these threats and ensuing acts of violence is "The Extraditables." If at first many Colombians believed that the evils of drug trafficking were felt

---

[50] According to the Colombian Section of the Andean Commission of Jurists (CAJ-SC), 23 judges and lawyers were killed and one judicial official was forcibly disappeared because of their professional activities between June 1989 and June 1990. An additional 23 judicial agents were assassinated or disappeared during the same period, although it is unclear whether these crimes were motivated by their professional work. CAJ-SC, *Jueces y abogados perseguidos por el ejercicio de su profesión en Colombia, junio de 1989 a junio de 1990* (Bogotá: CAJ-SC, July 1990). Some of these attacks appear to be the product of political violence, especially when they seemed designed to prevent investigations or prosecutions of crimes committed by paramilitary groups, such as the murder of twelve judicial officials in La Rochela in January of 1989. Americas Watch, *The Killings in Colombia*, p. 97.

mainly abroad, this assault on the Colombian state and civil society convinced most Colombians that the danger lay primarily at home.

During 48 hours in August 1989, drug traffickers murdered three prominent Colombians and caused a shift in the government's response to drug violence. The spree of murders began on August 16, 1989, when the Extraditables murdered judge Carlos Valencia, a member of the Superior Tribunal for Bogotá and one of the country's most distinguished jurists.[51] Although the cartel had threatened Judge Valencia for his role in cases involving its members, he had refused to abdicate his duties as a magistrate. Two days later, on August 18, the cartel murdered Colonel Valdemar Franklin Quintero, the chief of police of the Department of Antioquia (the capital of which is Medellín). That night, the cartel murdered Senator Luis Carlos Galán, presidential candidate for the governing Liberal Party, in the course of a large campaign rally in Soacha, near Bogotá. The presidential race was only beginning, but Galán enjoyed a large lead in opinion polls.

These murders prompted President Barco to issue several decrees, in exercise of the extraordinary powers granted the Executive Branch by the state of emergency.[52] They also triggered initiatives by the United States Government, announced in a speech by President George Bush on September 5, 1989, which have come to be known in many Latin American countries as the "Bush Plan."[53]

Some of the Barco decrees were aimed at drug traffickers and their property. Decree 1860 established an abbreviated extradition process, using administrative procedures that bypass the Supreme Court. Decrees 1856 and 1893 established a procedure to confiscate property seized by military or security forces that was linked to or obtained from

---

[51] Judge Valencia, an advocate of judicial reform, was a vigorous supporter of human rights. He was also a member of the Colombian Section of the Andean Commission of Jurists, a respected human rights organization.

[52] See Rodrigo Uprimny, "Las otras caras de la guerra a la mafia" in Comisión Andina de Juristas Sección Colombiana, *Informativo Legislativo y Jurisprudencial*, Vol. I, No. 3 (Bogotá: February 1990), pp. 102-105 & 162-164.

[53] The Bush Plan and its effects on human rights are discussed in more detail in Chapter VIII.

drug trafficking or production activities. Decree 1895 established prison terms for those who profit from illicit activities related to investment of drug traffic profits. Finally, Decree 1896 ordered the destruction of all aerial landing strips not licensed by Colombia's Civil Aeronautics Department.

The government also moved to bolster resources and protection available to public officials responsible for implementing the anti-drug-trafficking initiatives. Decree 1894 allows the Supreme Court to issue opinions on the constitutionality of state-of-siege decrees without revealing the names of the justices that voted to affirm or to nullify those decrees. Decree 1966 established similar secrecy requirements for the decisions of the Tribunal de Orden Público, which hears criminal appeals affecting insurgents, paramilitary groups and drug traffickers. Decrees 1855 and 1965 created special accounts and exempted specialized courts and the Executive Branch of existing restrictions in the use of allocated funds.

In the rush to respond to the murders, the government also issued other decrees that bear no relationship to the drug trafficking threat. Decree 1857 raised the prison terms for rebellion and sedition, the classic "political crimes" that are generally used against insurgent groups. It also repealed a Penal Code provision by which offenses committed in combat would only be punished as rebellion or sedition. Decree 1858 raised the penalties for threats against voters. Other decrees included in this package raise serious due process concerns. Decree 1859, for example, grants officials in charge of anti-drug-trafficking or counter-insurgency operations the authority to place persons in incommunicado detention for seven working days. Decree 1863 allows military judges, who are not part of the civilian judiciary, to order searches in the course of investigations into any crime. Decree 2013 permitted the government for reasons of public order to suspend popularly elected mayors and replace them with military officers.[54]

Under Colombian law, decrees issued pursuant to a state of siege are automatically subjected to an expedited Supreme Court review on constitutional grounds. On October 3, 1989, the Court struck down Decree 1893 regarding the procedure to confiscate property used for or obtained as a result of illicit activities. Decree 1893 contemplated an abbreviated procedure in which owners had five days to demonstrate that the property had not been used for drug trafficking or purchased with drug revenues. The Court ruled that the confiscation could not occur independently of a determination of guilt on the drug-related charges. On October 20, 1989, the government made the required amendment and issued Decree 2390. The decree authorized confiscation of a defendant's illicit property following conviction for drug trafficking or illicit enrichment. Confiscation can also occur if someone else is convicted of "fronting" for the real owners.

Significantly, the Supreme Court upheld one controversial aspect of the confiscation procedure contained in both Decrees 1856 and 1893—a shift to the defendant of the burden to prove the legitimacy of ownership and use. Since confiscation is a criminal sanction, we believe that forcing a defendant to prove his innocence runs counter to basic principles of criminal due process.

Also on October 3, the Supreme Court declared Decree 1863 unconstitutional because it did not specify the offenses for which military judges were authorized to issue search warrants. By then, however, the government had already amended this omission with Decree 2103 of September 14, 1989, which made clear that this power was limited to crimes of drug trafficking, crimes included in the Anti-Terrorist Statute (Decree 180 of 1988), and the so-called "political crimes" of rebellion, sedition, *asonada* (mutiny) and conspiracy. The Court has let this revised

---

[54] This last decree provoked an outcry among elected mayors. The government repealed it but then created *jefaturas militares* (military commands), headed by military chiefs with broad powers, in Pacho, Puerto Boyacá, La Estrella and Evigado, municipalities with serious problems of public order. (The Urabá region had been under a *jefatura militar* since 1988.) All but two of the *jefaturas* were abolished in August 1990.

decree stand, as it has with the other emergency measures described above (even though a similar extradition procedure had been struck down in previous years).

The extradition decree establishes an abbreviated procedure for processing requests from foreign governments. Detainees awaiting extradition are not eligible for conditional release. They are afforded a hearing to dispute the basis of the extradition request, but that hearing takes place solely before administrative bodies. No judicial review of an extradition order is allowed. Even though the extradition process itself does not result in a final determination of guilt or innocence, it results in a substantial deprivation of liberty. To avoid arbitrary deprivations, it is necessary that the matter be reviewed by an impartial tribunal. Particularly with as emotionally charged an issue as the pursuit of drug traffickers, Americas Watch believes that this impartiality can only be ensured by courts that are independent of the Executive. Review by such courts should include basic guarantees of due process, including the opportunity to be heard, to challenge the evidentiary and legal bases of the *prima facie* case brought by the foreign government, and to claim protection from extradition on grounds of domestic and international law. Insofar as the Colombian extradition process shields its decisions from judicial review, we believe it is fundamentally at odds with the due process requirements of the international law of human rights.

We are also disturbed that other serious restrictions on due process have been incorporated into Colombian law. To authorize incommunicado detention by security personnel for seven working days is, in our view, to invite the infliction of torture in the course of interrogation. Since no judicial authority is responsible for a prisoner's whereabouts during incommunicado detention—which can be extended to 18 consecutive days—it creates a very dangerous period during which the prisoner can be made to disappear. The period of imprisonment before a court assesses the grounds for detention can extend to nine or ten consecutive days under the decree. Only after a minimum of nine consecutive days in detention will the prisoner be placed under the responsibility of a judge, who then has three more days (six if there is more than one defendant) to receive his statement. The court then has an additional five days to rule on whether there is enough evidence to indict the prisoner or to order his release, for a total of 18 working days in a multi-defendant case. There is no *habeas corpus* during this period for arrests under the decree. If an application for habeas corpus is filed on the first day following this period, the requirements of Decree 182 of 1988 (discussed below) will delay a ruling on it for at least another 4 or 5 working days. The administrative detention of a suspect can easily be extended to 26 or 27 days.[55]

In declaring Decree 1859 constitutional, the Supreme Court ruled on October 3, 1989, that the decree suspended the obligation of police to notify courts of arrests within 24 hours. The Court also clarified that the police's powers to arrest under this decree applied only to persons captured in the act of committing a crime or to those with pending arrest warrants.

In authorizing searches by military judges the decree dispenses with the requirement of probable cause: a military judge can order a search on mere suspicion, and he need not provide any foundation for it. The same is true of warrantless arrests made by military or police personnel. Although the international law prohibition of arbitrary arrest may be suspended during a state of emergency,[56] it would have been wise for the Barco administration to impose strict obligations on the public officials who are given such sweeping powers, in light of the frequent practice of torture and disappearances by security forces in Colombia.

The initiatives to protect judges are undoubtedly necessary, given the systematic targeting of magistrates by drug traffickers and paramilitary killers. We are, however, skeptical that their security can be

---

[55] Uprimny, "Las otras caras de la guerra a la mafia," *Informativo Legislativo y Jurisprudencial*.

[56] Article 27, American Convention on Human Rights, allows suspension "in time of war, public danger or other emergency that threatens the independence or security of a State Party;" Article 4, International Covenant on Civil and Political Rights, permits suspension "in time of public emergency which threatens the life of the nation." It must be noted, however, that under Colombian law the suspension of the right not to be arbitrarily arrested is narrower than in international law: Article 28 of the Colombian Constitution allows arrest by the Executive Branch during a public order crisis, but states that the Executive must release those so arrested within ten days, or charge them and place them under the authority of the courts.

enhanced by keeping their identities secret. The creation of special courts that follow abbreviated procedures, with restrictions on defense counsel, reviewed by appellate judges with no names and no direct contact with the evidence, begins to make serious inroads into basic principles of the independence of the judiciary and due process.

Unfortunately, the trend toward due process shortcuts did not begin in August 1989. In January 1988, President Barco issued Decree 182, which severely limited the availability of *habeas corpus* relief.[57] This decree was issued in the wake of a public scandal over the perceived abuse by drug traffickers of the benefits of a democratic society, sparked by the use of a *habeas corpus* writ by Jorge Luis Ochoa, a Medellín cartel leader, to obtain release from the Modelo prison in Bogotá. Since then, according to human rights practitioners, *habeas corpus* relief has been practically unavailable in a country where it could go a long way to prevent disappearances and torture.

Parallel with the August 1989 decrees, the government launched an energetic law enforcement campaign against the cartels, with apparently widespread public support. By August 29, barely ten days after the three high-profile murders, 11,000 suspects had been arrested, 467 buildings had been searched and seized, and the government had taken possession of 1,313 vehicles, more than 1,000 weapons, 28 boats, 346 aircraft and 28,521 animals. Most of the 11,000 detainees were soon released for lack of evidence connecting them to drug trafficking. The large number of detentions suggests that a very wide net was cast, without particular regard for standards of probable cause. The suspension of the internationally-recognized guarantee against arbitrary detention should not allow the abusive practice of massive detentions.

---

[57] Decree 182 establishes the mandatory referral of a *habeas corpus* petition to the prosecuting attorney when the detainee is held for either drug-trafficking or insurgency offenses. His opinion is not binding, but the judge cannot issue a writ without hearing him. For all other *habeas corpus* applications, judges must inquire of the security forces whether the petitioner is sought or charged in connection with drug traffic or political crimes. Further restricting the availability of this important safeguard, applications can now be filed only before "superior courts" which exist only in the larger cities; municipal judges no longer hear them.

The policy shift following the August crisis also reversed several positive steps previously taken by the Barco administration.[58] The elite corps of police forces created in April 1989 to dismantle paramilitary groups and *escuelas de sicarios* was, according to most observers, redirected in pursuit of the heads of the Medellín cartel. This, of course, reflects the government's insistence that the crimes of the paramilitary groups are the exclusive responsibility of the Medellín cartel. The result has been that notorious paramilitary leaders who do not happen also to be major drug traffickers, like Fidel Castaño, Henry Pérez and Luis Rubio, are not being actively sought, despite their continued political violence against leftist activists and their perceived *campesino* supporters.

In a few cases at the beginning of 1990, the elite police corps has been used in counterinsurgency operations, according to human rights organizations. On January 5, members of the elite corps battled an ELN group in Cúcuta, Norte de Santander department. One police officer and two guerrillas died in the confrontation.[59] On January 25, the corps engaged an ELN cell, this time in Tubará, Atlántico. One ELN member was injured in the skirmish and two civilians were detained.[60] The elite police corps has committed serious abuses in pursuit of drug traffickers. In June 1990, several Medellín-based human rights organizations charged the corps with massive and indiscriminate arrests, especially among youths in poor neighborhoods. The human rights monitors also noted that gangs sponsored by drug traffickers (of which there are 86 in Medellín alone) reacted to the pressure by singling out policemen of the corps for murder. According to the human rights organizations, the corps retaliated by seeking gang members at night in bars and meeting places, kidnapping them and murdering them, giving rise to a spiral of vendettas in which many innocent citizens were also

---

[58] *News from Americas Watch*, "Colombian Government Adopts Measures to Combat Paramilitary Death Squads."

[59] Comisión Intercongregacional de Justicia y Paz, *Justicia y Paz*, p. 24.

[60] Ibid., p. 26.

caught.[61]   In press releases circulated in 1990, the Extraditables accused the corps of arresting their members and causing them to disappear (see our discussion of those allegations in Chapter V).

Americas Watch believes that it is a serious mistake to direct the elite police corps against an ever-widening array of objectives, because its operational capacity against the paramilitary groups is thereby reduced. The elite corps also runs the risk of infiltration and corruption by those forces (including drug lords) interested in fighting the social base of the guerrillas, and of becoming an instrument of the regional brigades of the Army involved in "dirty war" tactics.

The Barco government proclaimed that it was fighting a "war" against drug trafficking, which it equated with a struggle for the survival of democracy.[62]   The use of such dramatic terminology may be helpful in gathering popular support, but it carries the risk that controversial measures will be justified as part of the war effort, such as the sacrifice of important civil liberties. The debate over these policies is also tainted by this sense of urgency. In addition, the terminology is not simple rhetoric: with the open support of the Bush Administration, the Colombian government has brought the Colombian military into the struggle against drug trafficking, and the solutions offered for the problem are increasingly of a military nature. Many observers have questioned the wisdom of giving the high-sounding name of "war"—with the implication that the adversary can be targeted and killed—to what is, in essence, a law-enforcement problem. Although Americas Watch is not in a position to pass judgment on the likelihood of success of the Colombian program in curbing drug trafficking, we are troubled by the human rights implications of an approach that raises the stakes of the confrontation to the level of a war for the survival of the Colombian nation.

The August crisis prompted the Colombian government to redirect its efforts in other areas as well, such as the caseload of the

---

[61] Organismos de Derechos Humanos en Antioquia, *Acción Urgente*, Medellín, June 26, 1990.

[62] "Colombia Cartels Tied to Bombing," *New York Times*, December 8, 1989; Douglas Farah, "Barco Defiant after Deaths of 52 in Blast," *Washington Post*, December 8, 1989.

Public Order courts.   In 1989, some Public Order judges had taken courageous initiatives against paramilitary violence, giving rise to hopes that the judicial system could make a substantial contribution to the suppression of political violence.[63] Since then, however, they seem to have lost their ability to deal with paramilitary violence, and no similar results have been produced.

The cartels retaliated against this campaign by declaring war themselves, in the name of the Extraditables, and claiming persecution against their families and discriminatory seizure of their property. A string of bombings of important enterprises in Medellín followed. In addition, the main offices of the Bogotá daily *El Espectador* were destroyed by powerful explosives on September 2, 1989. A similar attack was made against the offices of an important regional newspaper, *Vanguardia Liberal*, of Bucaramanga. The cartels also attempted to murder General Miguel Maza Márquez, the chief of DAS, and on December 6 destroyed a large part of the DAS headquarters in Bogotá, killing 70 persons.[64] On November 27, 1989, a bomb destroyed an Avianca passenger plane in flight near Bogotá, resulting in the death of more than 100 passengers. In mid-December, the cartel kidnapped the son of Germán Montoya, President Barco's secretary and key advisor.

The government's efforts seemed to yield some results: by early 1990, the price of coca leaves in Peru and Bolivia had fallen from two dollars a kilogram to less than 50 cents, which is said to be below the cost of production. Observers agree that the drop in price was due to the disruption of trafficking operations, leaving the cartels unable to provide planes to transport coca leaves and "basic paste" to laboratories outside the areas where coca is grown. This interfered with the principal role played by the Colombian cartels—the processing of basic paste into cocaine and the transportation of the finished product to consumer

---

[63] See Americas Watch, *The Killings in Colombia*. In Chapter VII of the present report we comment on the status of those cases.

[64] General Maza Márquez has been in the forefront of anti-cartel efforts, and has revealed their role in paramilitary violence.

markets in the United States and Europe.[65] The Colombian government also announced many arrests and the seizure of relatively large quantities of cocaine ready to be shipped abroad. The significance of these seizures is difficult to assess, however, in light of the uncertain volume of the cocaine trade.[66]

On December 15, 1989, the Colombian government struck the most devastating blow of its war on drugs. José Gonzalo Rodríguez Gacha, also known as "El Mejicano," and one of the three top leaders of the Medellín cartel, was spotted at a farm he owned near the town of Tolú, department of Sucre. According to official accounts, he was killed by police forces when he attempted to escape capture. Several members of his inner circle were killed with him, including his son Freddie, who had been captured a few days earlier, then released and followed to his father. The specific circumstances of Rodríguez Gacha's death remain murky, and the Colombian government has not clarified them. According to an article written by Peter Eisner, an American special operations team participated in the operation.[67] The death of Rodríguez Gacha was considered a significant blow to the drug traffickers not only because of his leadership position in the Medellín cartel, but also because he was widely considered to be at the center of the cartel's violent campaign against perceived opponents.

---

[65] It should be noted, however, that while the price of coca leaf dropped, the price of cocaine in consumer markets remained the same, which could well result in a large profit windfall for the cartels. It is clear, in any event, that these indicators cannot be interpreted as making the illicit drug trade any less profitable.

[66] A report by the Government Operations Committee of the U.S. House of Representatives, while generally critical of the Bush Administration's drug-interdiction efforts, gave high marks to the role played by Colombian officials. *Stopping the Flood of Cocaine with Operation Snowcap: Is it Working?, Thirteenth Report by the House Committee on Government Operations (together with Additional Views)* (Washington, D.C.: GPO, August 1990).

[67] *Newsday*, May 4, 1990. The Bush administration denied that any U.S. troops were involved in the operation. Michael Wines, "U.S. Says It Aided Bogotá Drug Raid," *New York Times*, May 5, 1990; "Cheney: No role in death of drug lord," *Miami Herald*, May 5, 1990.

His killing came at a time when most observers believed that Barco's anti-trafficking efforts were failing and that only a big catch would make them a success.   But even following Rodríguez Gacha's death, Colombian and American drug-interdiction experts are not claiming victory.   Despite the previously noted disruption in operations around coca-growing areas, the cocaine trade has not been interrupted. It is also unclear whether the drop in prices of coca leaves is permanent. As for the operation of paramilitary groups, Rodríguez Gacha's death has had no discernible effect.   Either the Medellín cartel was quick to replace "El Mejicano" as the mastermind and financier of these groups, or these gangs of killers are not sponsored exclusively by the drug traffickers.[68] Whatever the reason, it has already been noted that paramilitary violence increased sharply in the first half of 1990, including the murder of two leftist presidential candidates.

Throughout the "war" on drugs, leading drug traffickers responded with a combination of terrorist violence and offers to negotiate.   The Barco government pledged publicly never to enter into a dialogue with the drug traffickers.   As the human cost of the policy mounts, however, many influential Colombians have called for some sort of negotiated solution.   It appears that the cartel leaders' key demand is an end to extradition to the United States; they have even offered to surrender to Colombian authorities and serve sentences imposed by Colombian judges.   Presumably, they would also insist on retaining control over vast property interests they have purchased over the years. Although the Barco administration adamantly denies it, many observers believe that there have been secret, informal contacts between the government and cartel agents, particularly after the cartels kidnapped the son of Germán Montoya.   The young Montoya was released unharmed on January 22, 1990 in Bogotá.

In one of his early acts in office, President Gaviria partially retreated from Barco's extradition strategy.   On September 5, 1990, Gaviria promulgated Decree 2047 that allows persons accused of drug

---

[68] As explained in Chapter II, Americas Watch shares the assessment of many Colombian observers that the Medellín cartel plays a large role in paramilitary violence, but that a complex web of support and sponsorship from other powerful sectors also plays a role.

trafficking to turn themselves in, provide intelligence on their accomplices and relinquish property earned illegally. In exchange, the government promises immunity from extradition and a reduction by half of sentences imposed by Colombian courts. The purpose in backing away from the extradition strategy is, according to press reports, to create an incentive for lower and middle-ranking traffickers to break away from their seniors.[69] At the time of this writing it is still too early to tell whether the new strategy is working.

In late August, 1990, the Medellín cartel kidnapped Francisco Santos, chief news editor of *El Tiempo*, Diana Turbay, editor of *Hoy por Hoy* magazine and daughter of former President Julio César Turbay Ayala, and five other journalists, one of them of German origin. The kidnappers did not ask for money or make any other demands, and as of this writing, six weeks after their abduction, the journalists are still being held. On Friday, October 5, 1990, four distinguished personalities offered their services as a mediation team to help release the captive journalists. They are former presidents Alfonso López Michelsen and Misael Pastrana Borrero, Cardinal Mario Revollo Bravo and Diego Montaña Cuéllar, a member of Congress and former leader of the Unión Patriótica. The government immediately announced that it welcomed the mediation effort "as a humanitarian gesture," but insisted that it will not engage in negotiations with the Medellín cartel.[70]

Since the death of Rodríguez Gacha, the government has pointed to Pablo Escobar as the most prominent leader of the cartel who is still at large.[71] In recent months, government officials have claimed that they have Escobar on the run, and that they have nearly apprehended him more than once. The government has stated that top assistants to

---

[69] Arana, "Colombia changes course...," *Miami Herald*; Farah, "Colombia Offers...," *Washington Post*.

[70] Andrés Oppenheimer, "Colombia accepts mediation effort," *Miami Herald*, October 7, 1990.

[71] Carlos Lehder, a reputed leader of the Medellín cartel in its early years, was extradited to the United States in February 1987 and is serving a prison sentence in the maximum-security facility in Marion, Illinois.

Escobar have been captured or killed in action.[72] At the same time, government officials blame Escobar for virtually all of the crimes that have taken place in the first half of 1990.   The evidence for the government's claim is discussed in Chapter II; we note here that the Extraditables, which seem to be under Escobar's control, have claimed responsibility for some of these violent acts, while denying any involvement in others. Many observers interviewed by Americas Watch expressed skepticism about the government's charge that Escobar and the Medellín cartel are responsible for the murder of presidential candidates Bernardo Jaramillo and Carlos Pizarro. We discuss the available evidence on those cases in Chapter V.

In the view of Americas Watch, the Barco government, by blaming Escobar for all terrorist actions against the state and the left, seriously misrepresented the nature of political violence in Colombia. The characterization ignores the role of powerful economic sectors and well-placed agents of the state in political violence. Until the government acknowledges its own role in particular, it will be powerless to control the violence.

The Colombian war on drugs continues as of this writing. It has taken a large human toll, but it also seems to have yielded some results. No one, however, is willing to predict when the war might come to an end.   Americas Watch recognizes that, for domestic as well as international reasons, the Colombian government must give a high priority to the pursuit of these powerful criminal organizations. For the

---

[72] Official statements claim that, on June 13, 1990, one of Escobar's military leaders, John Jairo Arias, was killed in a shootout with the authorities. In early July 1990, the Colombian military began their so-called "Apocalypse" operation to apprehend Escobar. During the operation, which employed approximately 500 agents of the elite police corps and an additional 1500 army troops, 25 of Escobar's agents were arrested, including Hernán Darío Henao Quintero, Otoniel González Franco, Carlos Taborda Pérez and Julio Javier Betancur Vélez. Douglas Farah, "Drug Lord's Base Hurt, Officials Say," *Washington Post,* July 15, 1990; and Ana Arana, "Colombia on Trail of Drug Lord," *Miami Herald,* July 12, 1990. On August 11, Escobar's cousin and right-hand man, Gustavo de Jesús Gaviria, was killed in a shootout with the elite police corps in his apartment in Medellín. Douglas Farah, "Colombian Police Claim a Major Blow to Cartel, *Washington Post,* August 13, 1990.

reasons explained above, however, we are seriously concerned by the approach taken by the Barco administration because of its erosion of fundamental rights. In this regard, we agree with those in the Colombian human rights movement who see in this "war" a dangerous legitimation of authoritarianism, as well as a threat to important initiatives such as the peace process and constitutional reform.[73] We are also concerned that the single-minded pursuit of drug-traffickers detracts from the government's responsibility for addressing the long-standing pattern of political violence committed—or acquiesced in—by agents of the state.

---

[73] Uprimny, "Las otras caras de la guerra a la mafia," *Informativo Legislativo y Jurisprudencial* and also: Rodrigo Uprimny, "Guerra al narcotráfico, reforma constitucional y proceso de paz," *Informativo Legislativo y Jurisprudencial*, pp. 113-118.

IV. Violations of the Laws of War

While the bloody confrontation with the drug cartels has received intense international attention, the long-standing insurgency led by several guerrilla organizations continues behind the headlines. As discussed in Chapter VII, protracted government negotiations with one rebel organization, the Movimiento 19 de Abril (M-19), yielded an agreement for it to give up the armed struggle and join the political process. Several other organizations, however, continue to conduct military operations in several parts of the country and at least three of them are considerably larger and more powerful than the M-19. Political violence, thus, remains at high levels.

The Colombian military's response to the insurgency did not change in the period covered by this report. As a result, the number of combat casualties continues to be among the highest in the continent, and other aspects of the counterinsurgency effort have claimed an unacceptable number of innocent lives and unduly disrupted civilian society.[74] The Colombian armed forces dedicate a substantial portion of their troops and firepower to the confrontation with the guerrillas. In most places, this involves not only combat but also intelligence-gathering among peasants and covert operations to detect and capture guerrilla fighters and their civilian supporters. These covert operations frequently go beyond legitimate counterinsurgency methods to include forced disappearance and murder. For their part, the guerrillas continue to finance their operations through kidnapping, extortion and "tax collection" among civilians in areas where they operate. While they do target uniformed troops of the military and police, they also use force

---

[74] Preliminary statistics for the first three months of 1990 indicate that combat action claimed 262 lives (139 guerrillas, 112 military or police and 13 civilians) and left 129 wounded. Comisión Intercongregacional de Justicia y Paz, *Justicia y Paz*, p. 83.

against civilian authorities and political figures whom they consider enemies.

Americas Watch monitors violations of the laws of war by both sides to the conflict, as we do in other countries where there is an ongoing insurgency. In judging the behavior of each party we apply common Article 3 of the Geneva Conventions of 1949, which sets forth the minimum standards that govern a conflict not of an international character:

> [E]ach party to the conflict shall be bound to apply, as a minimum, the following provisions:
>
> (1) Persons taking no active part in the hostilities, including members of armed forces who have laid down their arms and those placed hors de combat by sickness, wounds, detention, or any other cause, shall in all circumstances be treated humanely, without any adverse distinction founded on race, color, religion or faith, sex, birth or wealth, or any other similar criteria.
>
> To this end, the following acts are and shall remain prohibited at any time and in any place whatsoever with respect to the above-mentioned persons:
>
> (a) violence to life and person, in particular murder of all kinds, mutilation, cruel treatment and torture;
>
> (b) taking of hostages;
>
> (c) outrages upon personal dignity, in particular, humiliation and degrading treatment;
>
> (d) the passing of sentences and the carrying out of executions without previous judgment pronounced by a regularly constituted court affording all the judicial guarantees which are recognized as indispensable by civilized peoples.
>
> (2) The wounded and sick shall be collected and cared for.

An impartial humanitarian body, such as the International Committee of the Red Cross, may offer its services to the Parties to the conflict.

The Parties to the conflict should further endeavor to bring into force, by means of special agreements, all or part of the other provisions of the present Convention.

The application of the preceding provisions shall not affect the legal status of the Parties to the conflict.[75]

Common Article 3 establishes clear, commonsense duties on all forces participating in an internal armed conflict. The article is explicit that its application does not convey any added legitimacy to the insurgent forces. In addition, while some guerrilla actions are compatible with the laws of war (as when rebels attack clearly military targets without the use of perfidious tactics), that does not make those actions any less punishable under Colombian domestic law. The duties imposed by common Article 3 are mandatory at all times; violations are not excused by the noncompliance of an adversary.

In this chapter, we address clear violations of the laws of war by all forces. The examples, however, are by no means exhaustive. These

---

[75] International Committee of the Red Cross (ICRC), *The Geneva Conventions of August 12, 1949*, Geneva, 1983. An Additional Protocol, known as Protocol II, was adopted in 1977 to provide a more complete codification of the rules applicable to internal war. Colombia has signed but not ratified Protocol II. Americas Watch does not believe, however, that the situation in Colombia satisfies the very demanding threshold requirements for the Protocol to be applicable. These set forth that Protocol II applies to non-international conflicts: ". . . which take place in the territory of a High Contracting Party between its armed forces and dissident armed forces or other organized armed groups which, under responsible command, exercise such control over a part of its territory as to enable them to carry out sustained and concerted military operations and to implement this Protocol." (Article 1, Protocol II; ICRC, *Protocols Additional to the Geneva Conventions of 12 August 1949*, Geneva, 1977). Although some Colombian guerrillas occupy extensive rural areas, where they enjoy some peasant support, their level of control of population and territory is not sufficient to meet the exacting standard of Protocol II.

violations often take place in remote areas of Colombia made even more inaccessible by the fighting. Fear of reprisal against witnesses, as well as the ordinary difficulties of collecting testimony in rural areas, has precluded a more comprehensive accounting. The practice of the Colombian police and military of routinely blaming the guerrillas for any violence in the countryside has also made objective monitoring more difficult. Colombia's non-governmental human rights organizations, to their credit, are making serious and consistent efforts to catalog human rights and humanitarian law violations by both sides and to publicize them.

Even with these complications, it is possible to discern clear patterns of violations by all sides to the armed conflict. In the following paragraphs, we describe these patterns and illustrate them with some examples. We begin with violations of the laws of war by the armed forces of Colombia, before moving on to violations committed by each of the major guerrilla forces.

A. Violations Committed by the Colombian Army

1. Abuses by Army-established self-defense patrols

Many abuses in rural areas are committed by self-defense groups organized and promoted by the Colombian Army. In large part, their actions and tactics are indistinguishable from those of paramilitary groups. Indeed, some paramilitary groups proclaim themselves to be civil-defense associations. Paramilitary abuses have been discussed at length in Chapter II, but it is worth repeating here that, particularly in areas of conflict, high-ranking officers of the Colombian Army provide paramilitary and self-defense groups with intelligence, protection and impunity, and thus share responsibility for their "dirty war" tactics. Civil defense groups, while conceptually different from paramilitary gangs, also include "dirty war" tactics in most places, usually under the direction—or with the acquiescence of—local and regional military commanders. In fact, it appears that the use of such tactics, mostly by men who are technically civilians, is an essential part of the Colombian Army's counterinsurgency strategy.

The Colombian Army continues to organize civil-defense groups in contested areas despite the clear prohibition contained in President

Barco's April 1989 decrees. For example, on a trip to the Magdalena Medio in May 1990, an Americas Watch mission obtained testimony from Emeterio Cala and his wife, María Lizarazo, both of Honduras Baja, municipality of El Carmen de Chucurí, Department of Santander, who said that, in October 1989, the Army urged peasants from the area to join a civil-defense patrol. The following is a summary of their testimony:

> The Army had set up a post in the Cala family's *vereda* (hamlet) in October 1989. A Lieutenant told each peasant that he should report every two weeks to answer questions about his neighbors. From the start, the officer also told the peasants that they should organize themselves. In October 1989, a meeting was convened in which the Army officers introduced the leaders of the *auto defensas campesinas* (peasant self-defense association). In the presence of the officers, a patrol leader named Ciro Antonio Díaz told the peasants that they must choose between joining the civil-defense group or leaving the hamlet, and that those who refused to join would be considered guerrilla supporters and killed. Emeterio Cala said that most members of the civil-defense group reside in the neighboring *vereda*, La Victoria. A few residents of Honduras Baja have joined the group, but the majority decided to leave the area. Some had returned by May 1990, but conditions remained very insecure.
>
> The civil-defense group is armed with assault rifles and carbines. Our witnesses did not know how the civil-defense members had obtained the weapons, but it is clear that they are being used with Army consent. Emeterio Cala was twice detained by the Army and accused of supporting the guerrillas. His 20-year-old son, Filemón Cala, had been arrested and beaten by Army Lieutenant Rolando Pulido in 1988, and accused of being a member of the ELN because—according to Lt. Pulido—"all students are ELN." In February 1990, following the murder of an ELN deserter, Filemón and his father were again accused of collaboration with the guerrillas by Army officers and the civil defense group. As a result of the threats, the family moved away from the area, although they tried to continue farming their small parcels of land.

On March 17, 1990, Filemón was captured at the family's plot by Ciro Antonio Díaz and several other civil-defense members. The patrollers trained their weapons on Filemón's small brothers and made them run away. Filemón's corpse was found days later, with a rope tied to his neck, a deep cut in his throat, and signs of horrible torture.

Ciro Antonio Díaz was later apprehended at the Bucaramanga airport and charged with possession of weapons. The Cala family made sure, through the local ombudsman (*personero*), that charges for Filemón's murder were also brought. As far as Americas Watch knows, no investigation is under way into the responsibility of Army officers for the actions of Ciro Antonio Díaz. According to the Calas, the civil patrol continues to operate in the area of El Carmen, and the others responsible for murdering their son are still at large.

Americas Watch received testimonies from other areas near Barrancabermeja, as well as from human rights monitors based in that city in the Magdalena Medio, which confirmed that civil-defense groups continue to operate in the area, supported and encouraged by the Army. The local Army contingents belong to the Luciano D'Elhuyar Battalion, which has established military and paramilitary bases in the region. The municipalities south of El Carmen are considered to be under the firm control of several civil-defense groups, some set up by the D'Ehluyar Battalion and some by the XIV Brigade in Puerto Berrío. In many of those areas, the Army patrols jointly with the civil-defense groups.

According to sources in the area, the civil-defense groups are remnants of MAS, an early paramilitary group established with the complicity of the drug trade.[76] Peasants in the area refer to the civil defense members as *masetos*, and the members themselves boast of their membership in MAS.

The Comisión Intercongregacional de Justicia y Paz, a human rights organization created by the Catholic Conference of Religious Men

---

[76] *Muerte a Secuestradores* (MAS) was the subject of the first report on Colombia published by Americas Watch, *The "MAS Case" in Colombia: Taking on the Death Squads*, July 1983 (New York: Americas Watch Committee, 1983).

and Women of Colombia, conducted a fact-finding mission in the rural areas of Santander Department in early 1990. A report of the mission provides evidence that civil-defense abuses, with Army complicity, have taken place not only in El Carmen de Chucurí but also in neighboring regions of the Department of Santander.[77]

Citing local witnesses, the report says that José Parra, a well-known MAS member who was in uniform and participating in a sweep with an Army patrol, killed Luis Alberto Suárez Saavedra, a 26-year-old evangelical, in front of his family, on December 12, 1989, in the vereda La Ye, El Carmen.

Troops of the D'Elhuyar and Nueva Granada Battalions occupied the vereda La Plazuela, in nearby Simacota municipality, on December 18, 1989. This was the third Army occupation of this vereda that year. Soldiers distributed pamphlets signed by a Movimiento de Autodefensas Campesinas de Colombia, eight months after such civil-defense groups had lost any vestige of legality. The soldiers forced the peasants to post the pamphlets under threat of reprisal. The peasants identify some of the uniformed soldiers as members of MAS who had made incursions in the area before. That same day, three men were held and brutally tortured; one was told that he was dealing "not only with the Army or police, but also with MAS." On December 21, all inhabitants of La Plazuela fled towards Barrancabermeja, leaving their crops behind.[78]

2. *Indiscriminate fire against civilians*

In pursuit of guerrilla strongholds, the Army conducts aerial strafing and bombing of rural areas. Strafing is generally done from helicopters equipped with machine-guns, and bombs are dropped from jet-fighter planes. Under the laws of war, these actions are legitimate if conducted against strictly military targets such as guerrilla camps or

---

[77] Fr. Javier Giraldo, S.J., Report (untitled), Bogotá: no publisher, March 8, 1990.

[78] Ibid., pp. 1 & 2.

contingents. If civilians voluntarily travel or camp with the guerrillas they are deemed to have assumed the risk of battle and their eventual death or wounding are considered collateral to a legitimate attack. Even if guerrillas attempt to shield themselves by placing themselves among civilians—a violation of laws of war in its own right—they may still be targeted so long as, under the "rule of proportionality," the military advantage to be gained from the attack is not disproportionate to the collateral civilian casualties. In all circumstances, the attacker is under a duty to minimize harm to the civilian population.

As the preceding paragraph makes clear, the laws of war leave abundant room for military leaders to operate within the confines of legitimacy. In operations in the Colombian countryside, however, the Colombian armed forces have recently violated their duties to protect civilians. Americas Watch has received complaints of aerial bombardment of rural areas in several different regions. In many cases, it is not possible for us to say without further information that the bombings violate the laws of armed conflict. Assuming a legitimate military target, the rule of proportionality does not require a parity of weaponry, so long as the weapon is not used in a manner that causes disproportionate civilian casualties. Nonetheless, before an aerial attack can be deemed legitimate, it is necessary to examine whether guerrillas were present in the area, whether the attackers should have known that civilians might be affected, and if so, whether some form of warning was given to civilians so that they could escape the path of battle.

In some cases, however, we have been able to conclude that attacks violated the laws of armed conflict. For example:

> At 5:30 a.m. on January 6, 1990, a slow-flying reconnaissance plane flew over the municipality of Yondó, Antioquia, which is across the river from Santander department in the Magdalena Medio region. It fired several flares to illuminate the area, allowing four K-Fir fighter-bombers to drop bombs at the vereda La Concepción. Immediately thereafter, five helicopters fired their machine guns at the roofs of the houses. There were no deaths, but several dwellers, including a woman and her two daughters, ages 6 and 9, were wounded and had to undergo surgery.

The following day, helicopters fired at the nearby hamlet of Bocas del Don Juan. Army troops were then flown in and occupied the villages for two weeks. When human rights monitors later visited the area, they found that the ground troops had burned down most houses in La Concepción, and stolen cattle and property from the fleeing peasants.

On January 10, 1990, a Colombian Navy unit fired at a canoe carrying eleven peasants fleeing the fighting, including six minors, in Caño San Lorenzo (jurisdiction of San Pablo, Bolívar department, near the hamlet mentioned above). Three of the eleven were killed and two wounded, including a small girl. That same night, the naval fleet captured a 26-year-old fisherman, Libardo Orduz, also in Caño San Lorenzo, stole his money and killed him after cruel torture.[79]

The Army officially presented this attack as a confrontation with the XXIV Front of the FARC. International observers who visited the area a few days later confirmed to Americas Watch that the attack was in hot pursuit of a guerrilla contingent which had engaged the troops in battle hours before, but that the guerrillas had passed through La Concepción and were no longer there at the time of the attack. The same observers told us that there was no basis to the Army's claim that only guerrillas suffered casualties, and that the houses destroyed were a "guerrilla camp."

On February 9, 1990, military aircraft and helicopters bombed and strafed the *veredas* El Cerro de la Aurora, Altogrande, Mirabel, La Tempestuosa, Vizcaína Alta and Aguadulce, in the area of San Vicente de Chucurí, Santander department. A skirmish with the XII Front of FARC took place the same day near Aguadulce. A FARC combatant claimed that the guerrillas had been observing a unilateral cease-fire but that they entered into combat in reaction to the attack on civilians.

---

[79] Fr. Giraldo, S.J. Report (untitled), pp. 3-4; Americas Watch interviews with residents of Yondó at displaced persons camp in Barrancabermeja, May 1990.

The next day, an A-33 fighter-bomber dropped bombs in the nearby area of Llanafría, which had been occupied since February 6 by airborne troops of the D'Elhuyar and Nueva Granada Battalions. Several *veredas* of the Llanafría area were again bombed on February 12 and 13, causing their inhabitants to flee toward the town of San Vicente de Chucurí. It appears that no civilian died in the bombing and strafing of San Vicente de Chucurí.[80]

In the episode described above, it is possible that the FARC contingent that was in the area was the target of both the aerial and ground attack. We have no way of confirming the claim by the FARC combatant that his troops entered into combat only to defend the civilian population. The bombing and strafing, however, affected many hamlets for several days and was not pinpointed to attack armed combatants; also the civilian population in the area was given no advance warning of the attack. Under those circumstances, it appears that the attack violated the obligation to minimize harm to civilians. In earlier incidents, the *veredas* La Plazuela, Caño Indio and Diviso, in the area of Bajo Simacota, south of San Vicente de Chucurí, were strafed by helicopters on January 28, 1989, causing damage to cattle but no casualties. On March 21, 1989, there were new strafing and bombing in the same place.[81]

Monitors who work with an organization called CEDAVIDA, which assists displaced persons in several regions of Colombia, told Americas Watch that the pattern of aerial strafing and bombing described above was repeated in other rural areas, specifically, in Putumayo, Guaviare and Caquetá. These attacks were also preceded by the flight of a reconnaissance plane, which the peasants call *El Bobo* (dummy) because of its slowness. The peasants told CEDAVIDA workers that they have learned to estimate the time they need to run away from bombs and, just before the bomb explodes, throw themselves to the floor, cover their ears

---

[80] Fr. Giraldo, S.J. Report (untitled), pp. 6-8; Comisión Intercongregacional de Justicia Y Paz, *Justicia y Paz*, pp. 30-31, 52.

[81] Americas Watch interview in Barrancabermeja with two community leaders from Bajo Simacota, May 1990.

and open their mouths. They claim that the explosion of 500 kilogram bombs, even at a certain distance, can throw them two or three feet into the air, and that the bombs leave very large holes on the ground.[82]

3. Abuses during ground sweeps in military operations

The aerial attacks described above take place as part of larger military operations, during which the Army occupies hamlets and towns and patrols the area in pursuit of guerrilla contingents. Many serious crimes are committed by Army troops during such ground operations, including murders, disappearances and torture of civilians and of enemy combatants placed *hors de combat* by their wounds or by surrender. As part of counterinsurgency operations, these abuses constitute grave breaches of Common Article 3.

> Catalino Guerra, a peasant from *vereda* La Concepción, was reported missing since January 6, 1990, when he decided to stay in the *vereda* as it was being bombed and later occupied by the Army.[83]
> Counterinsurgency troops arrested Germán Neira Mendoza and Carlos Sierra in the *vereda* Kilómetro 8, near Puerto Wilches, Santander, on January 3, 1990. The troops beat the two men and forced them to board a vehicle. They forced Neira to dig a grave and then tied him to a tree and kept him there for several hours. They then forced him to carry military equipment to a farm, and finally took him to a police station. Three days later, he was taken to the headquarters of Battalion Nueva Granada, where he was tortured and forced to give information on others. He was also forced to tell the Prosecutor that he was being well treated.[84]

---

[82] Americas Watch interview, Bogotá, May 1990.

[83] Comisión Intercongregacional de Justicia y Paz, *Justicia y Paz*, p. 19; Fr. Giraldo, S.J., Report (untitled), p. 3.

[84] Comisión Intercongregacional de Justicia y Paz, *Justicia y Paz*, p. 22.

Eliseo and Juan Caballero were two elderly brothers who were deaf and mute. They lived in *vereda* Altogrande. During the bombing of February 10, 1990, they failed to leave the house and escape with the rest of their neighbors. At the end of the bombing, Army troops approached the *vereda* and fired at the houses. They captured the two brothers, apparently tortured them, and murdered them. The corpses were found a few yards from their destroyed house.[85]

On February 12, Gilberto Peñaloza and Noé Quintero, who were working their land in *vereda* Vizcaína Alta, San Vicente de Chucurí, were murdered by Army troops during the military operation then in progress. Families found the corpses three days later, and claimed they showed signs of torture. In the *vereda* La Tempestuosa, Carlos Garavito was captured on February 9; his family saw him being forced into an Army helicopter. His body was found on February 20, completely destroyed under torture.[86]

On February 5, physician Juan Fernando Porras was arrested in a shopping center, Centro Comercial Cabecera, in Bucaramanga, and disappeared. He was a combatant in the ELN, which immediately kidnapped Senator Jorge Sedano, of the Conservative Party, to demand an exchange of captives. Porras's badly destroyed corpse was found in *vereda* Aguadulce, Llanafría, Santander, on February 23. He had been killed by four shots, and there seemed to be burns in several parts of his partly decomposed body. The body had been partially hidden in an area where the Army had been camping. Nearby were many empty packages of Army rations. An investigation into the murder is under way by the Office of Special Investigations of the

---

[85] Comité Regional de Derechos Humanos de Barrancabermeja, Americas Watch interview with monitors who visited the scene, May 1990.

[86] Comisión Intercongregacional de Justicia y Paz, *Justicia y Paz*, pp. 31-32.

Attorney General's office (Procuraduría).[87] The ELN released Senator Sedano unharmed two days later.

On March 9, in Santa Marta, Magdalena, a Colombian Air Force contingent fired at a boat that was sailing across the Ciénaga Grande, killing Antonio Espejo Guerrero, an official of the government's Institute for Renewable Natural Resources and the Environment (INDERENA), and wounding other members of his party. The official explanation of the shooting was that the boat had been confused with another one carrying drug dealers.[88]

4. Displacement

The actions described in the preceding pages forced thousands of Colombian peasants to leave their homes and seek refuge in nearby towns and cities. Nongovernmental organizations have been formed to assist them; in addition, popular organizations representing the *campesino* movement, such as the Asociación Nacional de Usuarios Campesinos (ANUC), have devoted considerable resources to tend to their needs. Members of these groups report that tens of thousands of people are living permanently as displaced persons in Montería, the capital of Córdoba department; lesser numbers can be found in other parts of the country. There are no official estimates of the war-related number of displaced. In Barrancabermeja, Americas Watch visited a neighborhood where peasants from Yondó and San Vicente de Chucurí are trying to resettle with assistance from several community-based organizations. We also visited a temporary refugee center in the same city, run by several church and community-based groups.

The funds for medical and food assistance for these people come from private sources. In the case of the emerging neighborhood of people seeking to settle in the city, the local government has provided

---

[87] Comité Regional de Derechos Humanos de Barrancabermeja, Americas Watch interview with monitors who were visiting the scene of the military operations and found the body, May 1990.

[88] Comisión Intercongregacional de Justicia y Paz, *Justicia y Paz*, p. 58.

some assistance, and funds for development projects have been contributed by the Presidency's Plan for National Rehabilitation (PNR), which was part of the Barco peace initiative, and has been continued under Gaviria. Some of these displaced have been harassed and briefly detained by the police, but they enjoy considerable support from the community of Barrancabermeja.[89]

As explained above, the Army forces these people out of their homes, either by unannounced bombing and strafing, or by the abusive behavior of soldiers and Army-sponsored civil-defense groups. But the Army provides no help with transportation or emergency care, and pays no attention to the needs of the displaced once they are away from their homes. This is a serious violation of the laws of war. It is not impermissible to displace people temporarily for reasons of imperative military necessity, but any force that causes such displacement is obliged to receive the displaced population in good care.[90] The force causing the displacement is also obligated to allow the return of the victims, and to assist them in that objective, as soon as the reasons of imperative military necessity are no longer there. But the Colombian Army has

---

[89] Some of the rural communities displaced by the war include Indian minorities; their plight is even worse because of the radical cultural maladjustment that results from their uprooting. The number of Colombians who are leaving the country to reside abroad either temporarily or permanently is growing at alarming rates. They are not forced to seek exile on account of counterinsurgency operations, but they certainly flee several different forms of persecution. Journalists, lawyers, human rights monitors and politicians have left Colombia after being threatened.

[90] Article 81, IV Geneva Convention Relative to the Protection of Civilian Persons in Time of War. Although this standard is meant to apply to wars of an international character, it is well-established that it applies as well to forced displacement in a Common Article 3 situation, in the absence of more specific standards. See for example, the following reports by Americas Watch: *The Miskitos in Nicaragua, 1981-1984*, November 1984; *Draining the Sea: A Report on Human Rights in El Salvador*, March 1985; *Violations of the Laws of War on Both Sides in Nicaragua, 1981-1985*, June 1985; *The Continuing Terror: Seventh Supplement to the Report on Human Rights in El Salvador*, September 1985; *Settling into Routine: Human Rights in Abuses in Duarte's Second Year*, May 1986; *Violations of the Laws of War by Both Sides in Nicaragua in 1987*, November 5, 1987.

done none of this. Indeed, except for the role of the PNR in helping to develop work programs, the Barco administration took no interest in this serious social emergency.

5. *Other violations attributed to the Colombian Army*

Puerto Valdivia: In mid-April 1990 there was a confrontation between the Colombian Army and the FARC in the area between the *veredas* La Junta and Genova, in the municipality of Puerto Valdivia, in the southern part of Antioquia department.   According to neighbors, troops of the Girardot Battalion of the IV Army Brigade came to several houses immediately after this battle, on April 18, and took away five peasants: Horacio de Jesús Graciano Jaramillo, María Zenaida García, Luz Elida Duque, Ramón Evelio Ríos and a man known as Fabio N.   Their corpses were found five days later in a common grave in a farm called "La Esperanza." General Harold Bedoya, Commander of the IV Brigade, said that the five were guerrillas who had been killed in the confrontation with the Army.

The people of Puerto Valdivia conducted protest demonstrations to complain about this massacre, which they claim was the third in one year.   On April 29, Army troops forcibly dispersed a group attempting to interrupt traffic, and in the process shot and killed a peasant called Horacio Legarda. On May 4, prosecutors and investigative officials tried to visit several *veredas* in La Esperanza to investigate the massacre, but they were stopped by unidentified gunmen who opened fire on them. The officials requested protection from the central government and eventually arrived at the common grave with the help of an Army helicopter. The officials identified the bodies of the above-named peasants. All bore signs of torture and, according to a forensic report, three had been hanged. Also on May 4, four Army helicopters opened fire on the civilian population of Puerto

Valdivia, causing around 300 to flee and seek refuge in a school building.[91]

García Rovira: The Comité de Solidaridad y Derechos Humanos, a local human rights organization in the Province of García Rovira, Department of Santander, wrote a public letter to President Barco and other authorities on June 27, 1990, reporting that on June 7, the Army had murdered eleven peasants, including an elderly man and two teenagers, in a place called El Ramal, *vereda* Ilarguta, municipality of Macaravita, García Rovira, Santander. The killing took place in the context of a military operation against the ELN called Operación Marte, which had been conducted by the García Rovira Battalion, based in Pamplona. The day after the operation, Colonel Alfredo Rodríguez Velandia, of the V Brigade in Bucaramanga, issued a report claiming that nine guerrillas had been killed in combat while the Army suffered no casualties.

The human rights group stated in its letter that it had visited the site and established that the eleven dead were all members of the Burgos family, killed while unarmed, at around 2 p.m. on June 7. The Army refused to grant relatives access to the site for 24 hours. Then, a helicopter came and the bodies were shown wearing military-style uniforms. A military judge ordered the clothes to be burned before they could be examined to determine whether they matched the wounds on the corpses. The initials UC-ELN were found in the hats of some of the dead, and weapons had been placed in their hands, including a grenade in the hand of 87-year-old José Alfredo Burgos. Some of the bodies, however, had bullet wounds in their heads from shots at close range. The Comité's letter stated that more than 2,000 peasants attended the funeral of their neighbors.[92]

---

[91] "Comisión investigadora no pudo cumplir su misión," *El Colombiano* (Medellín), May 6, 1990; "Campesinos, no guerrilleros," *El Colombiano* (Medellín), May 8, 1990.

[92] Letter signed by Father Pedro Elías Joya Aponte and Dr. César Carrillo, President, Comité de Solidaridad y Derechos Humanos, June 27, 1990.

Trujillo: On March 29, 1990, there was armed combat between the Army and the ELN in the *vereda* Playa Alta, La Sonora, municipality of Trujillo, in the center of the Department of Valle. Minutes before the battle, the Army fired at residents and workers who were repairing a road as part of their community volunteer work, wounding three peasants and two municipal workers, all of them unarmed. According to testimony gathered by a group called Coordinación Nacional de Derechos Humanos y Damnificados por la Guerra Sucia (CONADHEGS), the Army experienced at least seven casualties in the course of the ensuing battle with the ELN.[93]   The human rights organization charged the Army with committing serious abuses in retaliation for those losses.

On March 30, the Army rounded up the inhabitants of La Sonora, insulted and threatened them with murder if they refused to reveal the whereabouts of the guerrillas. A peasant named Rigoberto Prado was arrested, tortured, and released the same day. On March 31, unknown assailants murdered José Porfirio Ruiz, the local police chief of the El Tabor township. The night before, Ruiz had been filmed accusing the Army of wounding the peasants and workers at Playa Alta, and he had refused to cover his face for he "did not fear telling the truth." On April 1, after electricity had been cut off in La Sonora, several uniformed armed men with assault rifles came into the village in three cars at around midnight and took away eleven residents, including a 59-year-old woman. Authorities have denied any knowledge of the fate or whereabouts of these detainees, even though the kidnapping took place in a highly militarized area.

On April 2, at 10:00 a.m., five heavily armed men went to two small factories in the town of Trujillo and forcibly removed five wood carvers, placed them in two cars and left in the direction of Tuluá. One of the wood carvers was seen by a

---

[93] CONADHEGS, "Dossier sobre Violaciones a los Derechos Humanos y al Derecho Internacional Humanitario en Trujillo, Valle, 1990," Bogotá, May 24, 1990.

witness a half hour later, as he and others were being taken from a vehicle into the headquarters of the F-2 (police intelligence) in Tuluá. One of the factories is less than a block away from the police building in Trujillo.

On April 17, Father Tiberio Fernández Mafla, parish priest of Trujillo, was abducted on the road between Tuluá and Trujillo, together with his niece, Ana Isabel Giraldo, and lay workers Oscar Pulido, an architect, and Norbey Galeano. Father Trujillo's corpse was found floating in the Cauca river on April 24, showing signs of torture, as well as several bullet wounds and numerous cuts, including one across his throat. His companions, the wood carvers and the eleven residents of La Sonora remain "disappeared" as of this writing. For the disappearances in Trujillo, the Procuraduría has formally filed disciplinary charges against Army Major Alirio Antonio Urueña Jaramillo, Police Major Alvaro Córdoba Lemos, Police 1st. Sergeant Luis Aníbal Alvarez Hoyos and Police Lieutenant José Fernando Berrio Velázquez. The case is pending.[94]

B. Violations Committed by the Insurgents

While the Colombian government and the Medellín cartel stepped up their violent attacks on each other, the activities of the Colombian guerrillas were momentarily pushed out of the limelight. It appears that the major guerrilla groups adopted different strategies in response to the drug-related "war." None of them openly supported the war against the cartels, despite many of their supporters having been the victims of cartel-supported paramilitary violence. FARC remained relatively quiet during the worst months of the drug "war," which allowed them to dispel rumors of an alliance with drug-traffickers. The EPL publicly called for a negotiated peace with the government and reached a truce towards the middle of 1990 (see Chapter VII); in the meantime, however, it remained fairly active in regions like Urabá and Antioquia department. The ELN displayed very active military operations in that

---

[94] *Hoy por Hoy*, July 31, 1990, pp. 21-24; *El Espectador*, June 23, 1990, p. 10-A.

period, and according to some observers, launched new and more violent attacks under the theory that in times of crisis it is best for a revolutionary group to launch an offensive.[95]

1. *Ejército de Liberación Nacional (ELN)*

The ELN was responsible for the largest number of violations of the laws of war in the period under study, as well as for the most severe abuses.

Targeted Killings

Bishop Jaramillo: On October 3, 1989, an ELN unit called Frente Domingo Laín-Comisión Omaira murdered the Roman Catholic Bishop of Arauca, Monsignor Jesús Emilio Jaramillo, who was 73 years old and had served the Arauca diocese since 1970. He had been kidnapped the day before in a place called Caño Caranal, on the road between Fortul and Los Chorros, in the heart of Colombia's oil region. The guerrillas also kidnapped Father Elmer Muñoz, who was travelling with the bishop, but released him unharmed a few hours later. The kidnappers told two seminarians who were also in the bishop's vehicle that they wanted Mons. Jaramillo to deliver a message to the government. Monsignor Jaramillo's corpse was found the next morning on the road between Panamá and Santa Isabel. He had been shot twice in the head with an assault rifle.

The ELN leadership criticized the murder as having been committed "outside the conduct and guidelines of the organization." The Frente Domingo Laín nonetheless took responsibility for it and accused the bishop of "obstinate interventionism" in the guerrilla group's affairs. It appears that his killers were opposed to Mons. Jaramillo's efforts at mediation, which they considered an alliance between the Church and the dominant sectors in Arauca. According to different accounts,

---

[95] Enrique Santos Calderón, "Guerrilla y 'paras': vuelve y juega," *El Tiempo*, October 29, 1989.

Mons. Jaramillo was a dedicated, hard-working religious leader who invested great energy in improving the working and living conditions of the poor in Arauca, and promoted peasant and popular organization to protect their rights.[96]

Other than the disclaimer noted in the preceding paragraph, Americas Watch is not aware of any action taken by the ELN leadership to redress this murder or to punish those responsible for it.

In May 1990, Enrique Morales Moncada, who on March 11 had been elected mayor of Labateca, Norte de Santander department, was murdered by a single assailant who shot him at close range with a handgun when he was at his office in the Liberal Party headquarters in Labateca.   The attack was attributed to the ELN because that organization had earlier in the same year killed three other elected mayors in the department of Norte de Santander: Ramiro García Velázquez, of Convención; Carlos Julio Torrado, of Abrego; and Pedro Julio Hernández Carrillo (name of the town not given).[97]

On January 5, 1990, the ELN kidnapped Ricardo Alfonso Castellar, the mayor of Achí, Bolívar, and apparently accused him of organizing paramilitary gangs. His corpse, with one bullet wound in the back of his head, was found floating in the Cauca river three days later.[98]   On February 3, 1990, Pedro Jesús Hernández, the Conservative mayor of Arboledas, Norte de Santander, was taken away from a school during an inauguration ceremony; he was killed less than one mile away, and a red and black ELN flag was found in the area.[99]

---

[96] Neftalí Vélez Chaverra, S.J., "La tragedia del sinsentido," *Cien Días vistos por CINEP* (quarterly supplement to *El Espectador*), No. 8, December 1989; "El ELN asesina a obispo de Arauca," *El Tiempo*, October 4, 1989.

[97] Santiago Liñán, "ELN asesinó al alcalde electo de Labateca, Norte de Santander," *El Tiempo*, May 11, 1990.

[98] Comisión Intercongregacional de Justicia y Paz, *Justicia y Paz*, p. 6.

[99] Ibid., p. 30.

The ELN murdered Darío Zapata on March 5, 1990, in El Dovio, Valle. Zapata was one of the few peasants who had agreed to serve on an electoral jury in the area.[100]

The ELN targeted elected officials and candidates in the regions where it operates, with the announced intention of disrupting elections. In Pitalito, Huila, for example, voting was suspended on March 11, 1990 because the ELN detonated an explosive on the road to Mocoa, Putumayo. On the same day, election-related acts of sabotage by the ELN were registered in at least ten locations in six different departments.[101] Under the laws of war, candidates, election officials and voters are civilians, and are thus impermissible targets of military action.

Murder as reprisal

In several cases discussed below, the ELN rebels killed civilians who refused to cooperate with them or were perceived as spying for the government. These murders violate the laws of war because, as unarmed civilians, these victims are inappropriate military targets and because, if the ELN is purporting to apply criminal sanctions, it is obligated to provide due process, including an impartial adjudicator. The "popular trials" occasionally used are a mockery of justice and no substitute for this clear obligation.[102]

The ELN is responsible for the murder of cattle breeder José Mogollón, in Toledo, Norte de Santander, on January 1, 1990. He was shot at his farm by assailants who stole 60 head of cattle and burned down some farm buildings. Farmer Luis

---

[100] Ibid., p. 62.

[101] Ibid., p. 78.

[102] For a detailed explanation of this standard in international humanitarian law, see Americas Watch, *Violation of Fair Trial Guarantees by the FMLN's ad hoc Courts*, May 1990.

Guillermo Ochoa and his foreman, Antonio Arango, were killed the next day in Salgar, Antioquia, by an ELN unit consisting of five men and two women, who also destroyed a coffee-processing building. According to reports, Ochoa had refused to pay the guerrilla tax, or extortion, known as *vacuna* ("vaccine"). The manager of an airport in El Banco, Magdalena, was murdered on February 28, 1990, by an ELN contingent; the guerrilla group briefly took the town and sought him, alleging that he had "stolen" money from the city coffers when he served as municipal treasurer. On February 1 of the same year, the ELN killed Mario Salazar and Marcelo Emilio Sánchez in Caucasia, Antioquia, accusing them of being Army informers. Invoking the same reason, the ELN killed four workers at the La Esperanza farm in Montería, Córdoba, on February 10, 1990. In Bolívar, Cauca, on February 20, an ELN unit of 40 armed men gathered 1200 residents of the town of Guachicono and, after making a speech, killed Roque Gómez and Giovanni Córdoba Ordóñez. On March 15, 1990 in San Pablo, Bolívar, the ELN killed a peasant named Jesús Galeano Valencia and left a pamphlet saying that the man was "an active member of the state intelligence services." On March 31, 1990, three men were found dead inside a vehicle in Bochalema, Norte de Santander, with an ELN sign explaining that they had conducted "kidnappings, blackmail and extortion in the name of the ELN."[103]

Kidnappings for ransom

Pedro Martín Berrocal, a Spanish citizen and bullfight entrepreneur, was kidnapped in Quito, Ecuador on August 9, 1989, and held for 250 days. He was released after prolonged negotiations when his family paid the ELN one million dollars in ransom. The initial kidnapping was performed by a supposedly Ecuadorian rebel group called "Montoneras Patria Libre" but, as noted, the ransom was collected by the ELN. The same apparent

---

[103] Comisión Intercongregacional de Justicia y Paz, *Justicia y Paz*, pp. 9, 33, 35, 39, 64 & 69.

"front" organization for the ELN kidnapped Scott Heyndal at the border between Ecuador and Colombia on April 28, 1990. Heyndal, an American citizen and an employee of a mining firm, was also released a few weeks later. Neighbors of his family in Peoria, Illinois contributed to his ransom.[104]

2. *Fuerzas Armadas Revolucionarias de Colombia (FARC)*

Murder and Kidnapping in Acts of Reprisal

Briceida P.V. de Moreno, Rebeca Moreno Palacios and Luis Antonio Triana were murdered by seven men, allegedly members of FARC, who accused them of being Army informants. The killings took place in the *vereda* El Potrero, La Palma, Cundinamarca, on January 5, 1990. In Ocaña, Norte de Santander, three men were found shot to death in the area known as Aguas Claras, with a sign stating they were "deserters of the FARC-EP." On March 20, also in La Palma, FARC killed peasants Eduardo Ramírez and Luis Carlos Melo at the *finca* El Porvenir, in the *vereda* Avivay.[105]

In Cimitarra, Santander, a unit of the XII Front of FARC killed Oscar Ramírez Osorio, owner of the Hacienda La Fe, on January 16, 1990. They also kidnapped Ramírez Osorio's son and a peasant who was in the house. Another rancher and his son, Domingo Rueda Guarín and José Domingo Rueda, were killed at the *finca* La Cruzada in Fundación, Magdalena, on March 29, 1990, apparently by the FARC.[106]

---

[104] "Por un millón de dólares," *Semana*, May 8, 1990.

[105] Comisión Intercongregacional de Justicia y Paz, *Justicia y Paz*, pp. 10 & 65.

[106] Ibid., pp. 11 & 67.

Attack on an ambulance

On March 23, 1990, units of the VIII and XXIX Fronts of FARC, operating in Patía, Cauca, on the road to Popayán, destroyed an ambulance owned and operated by the municipality of Balboa.[107] In the same attack, they blew up an energy tower and set fire to two trucks that transported fuel.

Ambulances and medical personnel are protected by the laws of war, even if used by an adversarial armed force, because they are designed to care for the sick and wounded. The energy tower and fuel transport, however, like the oil pipelines frequently targeted by the ELN, are legitimate targets under international humanitarian law, even though their destruction is a violation of domestic law, because they can contribute economically to the war effort.

3. Ejército Popular de Liberación (EPL)

Indiscriminate Killing

On January 7, 1990, peasants participating in a popular festivity in the village of Pueblo Nuevo, Necoclí, Antioquia, were attacked by several armed men belonging to the EPL. Six died and 13 were wounded.[108]

Targeted Killing and Kidnapping

In Planeta Rica, Córdoba, on January 28, 1990, the EPL killed landowner Henry Ardila, 51, who refused to pay them a *vacuna*. Betulio Plazas and Juan Bautista, cattle breeders in the *finca* El Rocío, Valencia, Córdoba, were killed by the EPL on February 5, 1990. Alberto Soto Sierra, foreman of the *finca* Las Gatas in Ayapel, Córdoba, was killed by joint ELN and EPL

---

[107] Ibid., p. 79.

[108] Ibid., p. 6.

forces on February 11, 1990. On March 26, 1990, the EPL again struck in Planeta Rica, Córdoba, this time murdering landowner Humberto Martínez on one of his farms in El Almendro. On March 19, 1990, in Fundación, Aracataca, Magdalena, the EPL kidnapped a former mayoral candidate; in the process, they confronted the police in armed battle, wounding two policemen.[109]

Three peasants, Rodrigo A. Jiménez, Domingo de Jesús and Angel S. González, were taken away from *hacienda* Mundo Nuevo in Carmelo, Tierralta, Córdoba, on February 17, 1990. They were killed, apparently by the EPL, at a site less than a mile from their abduction; the corpses bore signs of torture.[110]

Indiscriminate Fire

A peasant, Néstor Rafael Martínez, was killed on February 23, 1990 in Turbo, Antioquia, when an EPL unit fired at a civilian vehicle carrying a government official near a place called Alto de Mulatos.

On March 14, 1990 in Santa Bárbara, Caldas, Antioquia, the EPL used dynamite to attack a roadblock; one civilian died and another one was wounded.[111]

The roadblock might well have been a legitimate target under the laws of war, since roadblocks are always set up by armed police or military units. Nonetheless, the attack constitutes a violation of the laws of war. The fact that civilians were hurt and that no military casualties were reported suggests that, at the very least, the attackers fell short of observing their obligation to minimize harm to civilians.

---

[109] Ibid., pp. 12, 35, 36 & 66.

[110] Ibid., pp. 38 & 50.

[111] Ibid., pp. 40 & 78.

V. Murder, Disappearance and Torture

Where Chapter II described violations by paramilitary groups, outlining the responsibility of the Colombian state for these abuses, and Chapter IV addressed violations of the laws of war committed in the course of counterinsurgency operations, the following chapter describes human rights violations that have been committed in Colombia since 1989.

The events described here are traditional human rights violations in which government agents are more directly involved. These cases are frequent enough that they constitute a pattern. Attempts by the government and by prosecutors and judges to investigate and punish them have not significantly reduced their occurrence. Americas Watch believes that the Colombian government must be held responsible for the actions of its agents and, more particularly, for not doing enough to curb those actions. The military high command, in our view, not only fails to do enough to stop these actions, but on some occasions deliberately shields and protects their agents from serious investigations.

In some of these cases, the role of security personnel is in dispute, so we discuss the relevant facts. A dispute of this sort is particularly intense in the case of the murders of leftist presidential candidates Bernardo Jaramillo and Carlos Pizarro. We include them in this chapter because they are quintessential political murders, even though it is not entirely clear who ordered them killed and why. Their leftist politics suggest a range of people with a motive to kill them, including many security force personnel. Their inclusion in this chapter does not mean that Americas Watch believes that agents of the state masterminded their deaths; it does reflect, however, our belief that the Colombian government has yet to make a convincing case that the "intellectual authors" do not include agents of the state.

A. The Murder of Presidential Candidates

Colombian and international observers agree with the government that the Medellín cartel ordered the murder of Liberal candidate Luis Carlos Galán in August 1989. For the reasons set forth in Chapter III, we, too, endorse this view. The government has recently brought charges against gunmen who participated in the shooting, and the evidence shows that they were sponsored by the Medellín cartel.[112] There is also no doubt that the cartel ordered the attack on DAS headquarters, the attempt on the life of DAS chief General Miguel Maza Márquez, the murder of Judge Carlos Valencia and the bombing of *El Espectador*, as well as other similar actions.[113] In all of these cases, the motive is clear, and in most of them, the cartel took credit through its clandestine armed structure, the Extraditables. The government, however, has also blamed the Medellín cartel, specifically, Pablo Escobar, for other murders that have shocked the conscience of Colombians: notably, the killing of Bernardo Jaramillo on March 22, 1990 and of Carlos Pizarro on April 26, 1990. Most independent observers interviewed by Americas Watch viewed the government's explanation of these murder with skepticism.

Bernardo Jaramillo was the presidential candidate of the Unión Patriótica for the 1990 elections, and a member of Congress. A 15-year-old hired gun, Andrés Arturo Gutiérrez, fired a Mini-Ingram submachine-gun at him on March 22, 1990, at the Avianca Terminal of the Eldorado Airport in Bogotá. Jaramillo was entering the terminal with his wife to take a domestic flight to Santa Marta for a short vacation. He was hit five times and died shortly afterwards. His bodyguards wounded

---

[112] Douglas Farah, "Colombian: 'Israeli Aided Assassins,'" *Washington Post*, August 17, 1990. Significantly, this article cites top Colombian law-enforcement officials saying that they have found new evidence that the killers of Luis Carlos Galán were trained by Israeli arms dealer Yair Klein, who is a former Israeli government security agent. See Chapter II for Klein's connections with drug trafficking.

[113] See Chapter III.

the young assassin and he was arrested. Under Colombian law, the minor who killed Jaramillo may not be criminally prosecuted; he is presently being held in a special part of a maximum security prison.

Carlos Pizarro, presidential candidate for the M-19 Democratic Alliance, was murdered on April 26, 1990, on board a flight from Bogotá to Barranquilla, where he was heading for a campaign appearance. He was shot at close range by a hired killer, who in turn was killed by Pizarro's bodyguards. He was identified as Gerardo Gutiérrez Uribe, 21, of Frontino, Antioquia. The assassin used an Uzi machine-gun that had apparently been placed for him in the bathroom of the aircraft.[114]

Within hours of each murder, the government blamed them on Pablo Escobar. Immediately after both murders, Escobar denied any involvement. General Maza Márquez said his early attribution of responsibility to Escobar in the Jaramillo case was based on DAS interception of communications between the cartels, which referred to an imminent attack on a major leftist political figure. If that is the case, and given Jaramillo's prominence, it is fair to ask why the government did not adopt special protective measures, including the simple one of letting Jaramillo know that something might be afoot.

The attack on Jaramillo came only a few days after President Barco had dismissed UP complaints of attacks on its activists as electoral propaganda, and only two days after the Minister of Government (Interior), Carlos Lemos Simmonds, had called the UP the "political arm of the FARC." Even before Jaramillo's death, other UP leaders had pointed out that this remark could legitimate attacks on UP members. Human rights organizations and political movements demanded the removal of Lemos Simmonds, who resigned on March 24, two days later

---

[114] Comisión Andina de Juristas—Sección Colombiana, memo, Bogotá, April 27, 1990.

the killing.[115]   Given the history of persecution of the UP, which President Barco has acknowledged since 1986, Simmonds's comments sound at least callous, particularly in light of the very real pattern of killings of UP members in early 1990. In retrospect, the statements by Barco and his Minister were highly irresponsible because they contributed to the climate of impunity that made Jaramillo's assassination possible.

La Voz, the Communist Party newspaper, published an article stating that the father of Gutiérrez, Pizarro's killer, is a police informer in Medellín, and that Gutiérrez's brother is a police-academy cadet. Americas Watch tried to verify this information during our May 1990 mission, but was unable to do so. Government officials flatly denied it. At interviews with Americas Watch, government officials said that Gustavo Adolfo Mesa Meneses, also known as "El Zarco," a man who had been apprehended on April 5, 1990, was the link between both crimes and Pablo Escobar. At the time of our visit, formal charges against Mesa had not been filed; we were told that evidence was still being gathered.[116]

In late July, DAS provided the Colombian public with more detailed information about the Medellín cartel's responsibility for Jaramillo's murder. According to DAS, on March 21, 1990, in the course of a conversation that was intercepted and taped, Escobar ordered Mesa to kill Jaramillo. To implement this order, 200 million Colombian pesos were distributed through various bank accounts to pay for the contract hit. Transfers between various bank accounts were made with a beeper, leading to the movement of large amounts of money to three underworld figures: John Jairo Arias Tascón, alias "Pinina"; Luis Alberto Castaño Molina, alias "Chopo"; and Carlos Alberto Londoño Vásquez, alias "La Yuca." Arias is considered the coordinator of all groups of *sicarios*, while

---

[115] Grupo de Trabajo Internacional de Derechos Humanos, "Sobre la Violación de los Derechos Humanos en Colombia," press release number 2, Bogotá, April 1990.

[116] Mesa was then being held in connection with the murder of journalist Jorge Enrique Pulido. He is also accused of the murder of Colonel Valdemar Franklin Quintero, chief of police of Medellín, in August 1989; the bombing of *El Espectador*; and the murders of two Medellín employees of that newspaper. As of the writing of this report, Mesa has now been formally charged with planning and arranging Jaramillo's death.

the other two are suspected of involvement in the murder of Minister of Justice Rodrigo Lara Bonilla.

DAS claims that Mesa hired two youngsters who worked in a Medellín paintbrush factory, and arranged for them to be trained in the use of machine guns by a man known as "Joaquín," "Reinaldo" or "El Campeón," but who has not been otherwise identified. The two young men are Andrés Arturo Gutiérrez Maya, who later killed Jaramillo, and Gerardo Gutiérrez Uribe, also known as "Jerry," who was shot to death after killing Carlos Pizarro. The two Gutiérrez youths are not related.

According to DAS, Andrés Gutiérrez was led to believe that he would have support during the assassination and would be able to escape, although in fact his handlers intended for him to die in the attack, as evidenced by his Mini-Ingram submachine gun having been set up so that the magazine would fall off after the first round of bullets was shot. The young man was put up under an assumed name in a Bogotá hotel, while his handlers all stayed in safe houses and private homes, where it was much harder for the police to detect them.

Gustavo Mesa was apprehended on April 5, 1990. According to DAS, he had in his possession a handgun, a beeper used to communicate with Escobar and Arias Tascón, a car, a motorcycle and a large amount of cash. DAS later discovered that 325 million pesos had been given to Mesa, presumably to pay for this and other operations, through a bank account belonging to his girl friend, Sandra Patricia Valencia. According to DAS, it also appears that part of Andrés Gutiérrez's fee was paid directly to his family, which has suddenly improved its lifestyle, even though all family members are unemployed.[117]

DAS has not provided the same detailed information on the killing of Pizarro.

It is highly commendable of DAS to provide the information it has gathered to the public even though at this point it sheds light mostly about only one of the two cases. As far as we know, however, only DAS's conclusions, not the specific evidence supporting those conclusions, have been made available. Moreover, the information so far gives little insight into the motives that might have led the Medellín cartel to kill these two prominent politicians.

---

[117] "Magnicidios: Qué se sabe?," *Semana*, July 24-31, 1990.

More important, the DAS report is silent on a key element in each murder: how the killers were able to avoid security arrangements set up at the airport and inside an aircraft in flight. Only months before, the Medellín cartel had blown up a commercial airplane, so presumably security arrangements in Colombia would have been even stricter than they are elsewhere in the world. There has been no explanation of how machine guns could have been brought into the waiting area of a major airport or smuggled on board a commercial aircraft. Our point here is not to disparage the valuable information offered by DAS, but to point out that major areas remain unilluminated. Even if the cartel murdered Jaramillo and Pizarro, authorities must investigate the serious possibility that, as in other cases, the cartel acted with assistance from agents of the state who were in positions to facilitate the crimes.

Moreover, the *modus operandi* of the assassination is not necessarily conclusive on the issue of responsibility. The murders were not the work of paramilitary groups which we described earlier in this report as organized forces linked to the state security apparatus. Rather, they are more properly classified as murders by *sicarios*, or hired guns. But hired assassins are not used exclusively by drug traffickers. The murder of Alvaro Garcés, the mayor of Sabana de Torres, which we discussed in our 1989 report and again in Chapter VI of this report, illustrates the Colombian Army's use of *sicarios*. Investigations thus should not take the use of *sicarios* as a reason to limit the scope of the inquiry.

There are also questions of motive that should be explored. Jaramillo was on record against extradition to the United States, and thus agreed with the cartels on their principal concern. Galán, by contrast, was not only a strong proponent of extradition, but also had advocated stripping Escobar of the immunity he enjoyed as a member of the Colombian Congress so that he could be made to stand trial for a murder he allegedly committed in the early 1980s.

On the other hand, as a leading member of the UP, Jaramillo was clearly a target of paramilitary groups, some of which are sponsored by the Medellín cartel. Such paramilitary groups have killed hundreds of UP activists and leaders, including Jaime Pardo Leal, the UP presidential candidate in the 1986 election. Incidentally, Pardo Leal, Jaramillo and all UP leaders and activists have consistently opposed extradition on political and ideological grounds, and that fact has certainly not protected them from attack from the drug cartels. Despite Escobar's denial of responsibility, therefore, it would not be out of character for the cartel to have ordered Jaramillo's death.

As for Pizarro, on March 2, 1989, he initiated a peace process with the Barco administration that culminated on March 8, 1990 in the M-19's formal surrender of its weapons. On March 11, 1990, after campaigning for only two days, he captured eight percent of the vote for mayor of Bogotá. His campaign for the presidency was gathering momentum, particularly after the UP withdrew following Jaramillo's murder. Pizarro's successor, Antonio Navarro Wolff, finished third in the May 1990 election, with more than 12 percent of the vote—the best left-wing electoral showing in the history of Colombia. These developments might have made Pizarro a target for those trying to prevent the emergence of a democratic left.

Pizarro was also on record in opposition to extradition and in favor of negotiations with the drug cartels. Although years ago the M-19 had prompted a bitter confrontation with the drug dealers by kidnapping for ransom a daughter of the Ochoa family, M-19 members and sympathizers have not been targeted by cartel-sponsored paramilitary groups in recent times. Indeed, Colombian military leaders (and U.S. diplomats) have charged the M-19 with acting in alliance with the drug traffickers. By contrast, the M-19 has a history of confrontation with the Colombian Army, including daring attacks on military installations and the bloody takeover of the Palace of Justice in 1985. Accordingly, there would appear to be a greater motive to kill Pizarro among military leaders and right-wing elements than among the drug traffickers.

In interviews with Americas Watch, government officials argued that Escobar's denials of responsibility should not be given much weight. We agree that they should not be decisive, but we note that the Extraditables have publicly declared war on the Colombian state and have not denied their participation in several other, equally spectacular crimes, such as the murder of Galán and the attacks on DAS and on its chief. It is not clear why they would break with that practice and falsely disclaim a role in the Jaramillo and Pizarro murders.

Whoever may have ordered the murders, the circumstances of each are such that they could not have been committed without important assistance from well-placed agents to provide highly secret information about security arrangements for a presidential candidate as well as access to places like airports and aircraft that are subject to strict security controls. Pizarro's personal bodyguards were former M-19 combatants, but his security was coordinated with the DAS. It is said that his security chief, as a supposed security measure, had changed the flight for his trip to Barranquilla at the last minute.

For all of these reasons, Colombian observers (and at least one government official speaking off-the-record) have pointed to the possibility that responsibility for the murders of Pizarro and Jaramillo may lie with a right-wing clique, aided by agents of the state, particularly in obtaining intelligence and gaining access to secure public places. During a television interview on Saturday, May 5, 1990, General José Joaquín Matallana, a well-known retired officer who is an outspoken critic of "dirty war" tactics, said that he was under threat from a right-wing group that included retired Army officers. According to observers, the aim of such a group would be to ensure that there is no opportunity for left-wing movements to establish themselves on the political landscape. The observers we talked to readily admitted, however, that there is no concrete evidence of such a group, other than the fact that its existence would provide a plausible explanation for the murders.

For its part, the government has conducted what appears to be the beginning of a serious criminal investigation and, as noted, has offered detailed information on at least one of the two murders. However, the investigation is by no means complete. Among the areas where further inquiry is called for are the questions of how serious breaches of security in both cases occurred, and what role state agents had in facilitating these breaches.

B. Other Murders

Diana Cardona Saldarriaga, the UP mayor of Apartadó, in the Urabá region, was murdered on February 26, 1990. She had been appointed to replace a mayor who had also been killed, and she lived in Medellín, commuting each morning to Apartadó with heavy security provided by the DAS. On the morning of her murder, she left her house with people who identified themselves as DAS bodyguards. The real bodyguards arrived at her house 15 minutes later. UP members claim that very few people knew she was residing in Medellín, and that she would not have left her house with strangers, so she must have known at least one of her killers. In a letter to the Minister of Defense, the Attorney General asked how the murderers could have had so much information about Cardona's whereabouts and movements, which were a closely guarded secret.[118]

The Cardona murder is only one of dozens of murders of members of the Unión Patriótica in the period under study. Americas Watch has expressed concern over the murder of UP activists since 1985, when the movement began.[119] Over 1,000 of its members have been killed in that time. The rate of killings seemed to decrease in 1989, but accelerated rapidly in early 1990, in the weeks preceding the election. Sixty-eight such murders were recorded between January and May 1990 by the Centro de Estudios e Investigaciones Sociales (CEIS), which published a special report on the subject in April 1990.[120] CEIS attributes the increase in murders to the elections, a view consistent with the fact that 60 percent of the UP killings in 1988 were committed in the first quarter, again just before the elections of that year.

The increase in killings of UP activists contrasts with an overall decrease in politically motivated killings of all sorts from 1989 to 1988. In an interview in May 1990, Dr. Emilio Aljure Nasser, Presidential Counsellor for Human Rights, told Americas Watch that the decrease in 1989 was a sign that the government's efforts to curb paramilitary violence were having an effect. According to the most reliable statistics,

---

[118] Comisión Andina de Juristas—Sección Colombiana, memo, Bogotá, March 20, 1990.

[119] See the following reports from Americas Watch: *The Central-Americanization of Colombia?: Human Rights and the Peace Process, January 1986*; *Human Rights in Colombia as President Barco Begins, September 1986; The Killings in Colombia, April 1989.*

[120] Interview, May 1990. As a result of this report, the staff of CEIS received telephone threats at work and at home. Armed men loitered in front of their office for a few days. Letters by CEIS to human rights groups in Colombia, dated April 25 and 30, 1990.

the rate of politically motivated deaths decreased from 11 per day in 1988 (4,204 for the year) to 8 per day in 1989 (3,211 for the year). Needless to say, the numbers are still unacceptably high; in the hemisphere, only Peru approached that figure in 1989. There was a decrease as well in combat deaths (a subcategory of the figures for political violence) in the two years (from 1,083 to 732). The only category in which an increase in the number of killings was registered was for "murders for social cleansing" (targeting street people, prostitutes, drug addicts, etc.).[121]

Unfortunately the limited figures available for the first few months of 1990 suggest that the rate of political violence is again on the increase. For example, there were 154 UP activists killed in 1988 and 71 in 1989, but fully 68 in only the first four months of 1990. The number of massacres (defined as killings of more than five victims at a time) rose from 68 in 1989 to 64 in 1988, although the total number of massacre victims fell from 547 to 427, in part because there were no massacres in 1989 comparable to those of La Mejor Esquina, Urabá and Segovia in 1988, in which between 17 and 43 victims died at a time.[122] In early

---

[121] CAJ-SC, "Una peligrosa democracia en peligro: Derechos humanos y responsabilidad estatal en Colombia," (citing the Centro de Investigacíon y Educación Popular (CINEP) data bank and *Justicia y Paz*, Vol. 2, No. 4), Bogotá, undated bulletin. As noted the figures of 4,200 for 1988 and 3,400 for 1989 represent all politically motivated slayings. Not all of these, of course are attributable to government forces. Moreover, the figure includes combat casualties (which by definition are not human rights violations and may not ever constitute violations of the laws of war), murders attributable to the guerrillas, and murders committed by paramilitary groups.

[122] The figures in this paragraph are taken from a statistical analysis provided by Dr. Aljure Nasser's office; they are consistent with the statistics released by CINEP, *Justicia y Paz* and CAJ-SC. The murder rate in Colombia is at least as alarming as the figures for political violence. The National Police counted 21,000 homicides in 1988 and 13,000 in the first half of 1989. The killing for all of 1989 reached nearly 23,000, approximately 69 per 100,000 inhabitants. For comparison's sake, the murder rate is 5 per 100,000 in Switzerland and France, and 11.3 per 100,000 in the United States. Since 1986, murder has been Colombia's primary cause of death for males aged 18 to 44. See CAJ-SC, "Una peligrosa democracia...."

1990, however, the death toll for the Pueblo Bello mass kidnapping and apparent slaughter (see Chapter II) is more than 40 for that single case.

In light of these statistics, it appears that the effects of the Barco administration's efforts to stem paramilitary violence has been marginal at best. Indeed, after initially concentrating its efforts on political violence, the government has directed its attention mainly to violence by the Medellín cartel. Since August 1989, political violence as such has not been a high government priority, and the more recent increase in the rate of political killings seems to reflect this inattention.

C. Disappearances

On July 4, 1990, Alirio de Jesús Pedraza, a 40-year-old lawyer, was abducted in front of many witnesses in the Suba neighborhood of Bogotá, by eight heavily armed men in plain clothes. Two uniformed policemen tried to stop the operation, but allowed it to proceed when the armed men showed them certain credentials. Pedraza was a member of the Comité de Solidaridad con los Presos Políticos (CSPP), a human rights organization. He was abducted shortly after attending a CSPP meeting. Military and police authorities deny his arrest.

In August 1989, Carlos Arturo Ortega Chicunque and his brother, who had been in prison on political charges, were re-arrested by police immediately after their release from the Modelo penitentiary in Bogotá. Their second detention was not acknowledged and they remain disappeared to date.[123]

According to the statistics of the Consejería Presidencial para Derechos Humanos, the number of disappearances decreased from 1989 to 1988, from 210 to 137. The CAJ-SC and CINEP published the same figures.[124] Again, however, those gains may be only temporary: in the first quarter of 1990, the Procuraduría received four times as many

---

[123] Interview with José Humberto Torres, Secretary General, Comité de Solidaridad con los Presos Políticos, Bogotá, May 1990.

[124] CAJ-SC, "Una peligrosa democracia...."

complaints of disappearances as in the same period in 1989.[125] The 150 complaints received by the Procuraduría include the 42 persons who disappeared in a single incident in January in Pueblo Bello, Antioquia (See Chapter II). Even if that case is excluded, the number of disappearances in the first quarter of 1990 is at least three times larger than the same period in 1989.

Like the killing of UP activists, the increase in the number of disappearances in 1990 may reflect the escalated political violence in the context of the election. However, there is some evidence that forced disappearances have taken place in the course of operations against drug traffickers. A press release issued by the Extraditables charged that Fredy López Ospina and José Crisanto Retavista were arrested by the Elite Corps of the National Police in Envigado, Antioquia on March 28, 1990, but that the police denied holding them.[126] In the same statement, the Extraditables also accused the Elite Corps of the detention and disappearance of two brothers, Omar and Guillermo Perea Rivera, in Envigado; the Extraditables threatened to kill Senator Federico Estrada Vélez—whom they had kidnapped—if the Perea brothers were not released. To our knowledge, none of these people have been accounted for.

D. Torture

Luis Norberto Serna, a leader of the metal-workers union FETRAMETAL; Heli de Jesús Quebrada Trejos, a union activist at a Goodyear plant; Héctor Emilio Castro, president of the Goodyear union; Elizabeth Suárez, wife of Castro and member of the CSPP; Harold Roberto Ruiz Moreno, a member of the national leadership of the political movement A Luchar; James

---

[125] Interview with Jaime Córdoba, Procurador Delegado para Derechos Humanos, Bogotá, May 1990.

[126] Comisión Intercongregacional de Justicia y Paz, *Justicia y Paz*, p. 74. Human rights groups based in Medellín also issued a complaint, based on testimony from residents in poor neighborhoods of the city, accusing the Elite Corps of firing indiscriminately at young people in the street and in bars. Organismos de Derechos Humanos en Antioquia, *Acción Urgente*, June 26, 1990.

Lozano Arias, a union activist at the metalworks Siderúrgica del Pacífico; and six others were arrested in Cali in March 1990, in the course of searches conducted by the Third Army Brigade. The search warrants were issued by military judges. Those arrested were all taken to the headquarters of the Third Brigade, where they were brutally tortured. Suárez, the human rights monitor, was raped. All of them were subjected to beatings, the "submarine" (holding the head under water until near asphyxiation), fake executions, forced standing for hours, and threats against themselves and their families. They were blindfolded and deprived of food for several days while at the Army quarters. Serna was injected with an hallucinogenic drug.

Attorney Daniel Libreros Caicedo, who represented these trade union activists, was arrested at the Cali airport on March 27, 1990 by airport police and the intelligence section of the National Police. He was taken to DAS headquarters in Cali and held until April 6, when the Procuraduría General de la Nación (Attorney General's Office) ordered his release. The detained activists were eventually taken to the penitentiaries in Cali and placed under the jurisdiction of a Public Order judge. They have since been released.[127]

The victims in many of the other cases described in this report were also tortured. Americas Watch is aware of no statistics on the incidence of torture, but all observers and officials interviewed agreed that it is a pervasive practice. We have no reason to believe that the problem of torture has improved in any way since the publication of our last report.

The Extraditables have also charged repeatedly that police forces conducting the "war on drugs" use torture against suspects. They accuse the Intelligence and Judicial Investigations Bureau of the Police (DIJIN) of kidnapping, torturing and murdering more than 40 of their members, and the DIJIN Chief, Police Colonel Oscar Peláez Carmona, of ordering

---

[127] CAJ-SC, letter to Americas Watch, April 9, 1990.

massacres in Bogotá and Gómez Plata, Antioquia.[128] Unfortunately, the evidence that torture is used in the context of drug interdiction and extradition efforts is not restricted to allegations made by underworld figures.

Nelson Cuevas Ramírez was wrongly extradited to the United States in December 1989. In March 1990, a federal judge in New York declared him innocent, offered him excuses on behalf of the United States judiciary, ordered an investigation against prosecutors who had charged Cuevas, and allowed him to return to Colombia. Upon his return, Cuevas made statements to the Colombian press about mistreatment that he witnessed at DIJIN headquarters in Bogotá.

Cuevas reported that police officers use a room that they jokingly call "Jimmy's room," alluding to a popular television show for amateur singers named "Cante Aunque No Cante" ["Sing Even if You Don't Sing"] whose host is Jimmy Salcedo. In this room, prisoners are handcuffed and tied to chairs; bright lights are focused on them and earphones placed on their ears; the headpieces then carry a sound that is gradually amplified by their captors. The prisoners scream in pain. Cuevas also said that agents of the U.S. Drug Enforcement Administration (DEA) personally visit these installations frequently. He said that he was not subjected to the treatment, but he saw and heard it applied to others. He also claims to have seen prisoners returned to their cells with serious physical injuries.[129]

---

[128] Press communiqué dated March 28, 1990; *La Prensa*, March 30, 1990, p. 12. The Gómez Plata massacre took place on January 20, 1990; its victims were ten persons presumed to be members of a gang called La Ramada. The Comisión Intercongregacional de Justicia y Paz listed the case under the category of "social cleansing." *Justicia y Paz*, January-March 1990, pp. 13 & 14. The Extraditables made similar charges in communiqués dated April 4, 13, & 30 (in which they denied involvement in Pizarro's murder), June 13 and July 27 (in which they declared a unilateral truce).

[129] *La Prensa*, March 25, 1990, p. 13; *La Prensa*, May 6, 1990, p. 5. The latter article says that Minister of Government, Horacio Serpa Uribe, had ordered an investigation and had asked the newspaper to publish Cuevas's testimony.

VI. The Institutional Response

Colombians have not remained quiet in the face of the terrifying succession of abuses. Colombia's civil society continues to respond with courageous and intelligent initiatives in the quest for peace with justice. In particular, Colombia's diverse and rich human rights movement deserves credit for refusing to live with the terror and for demanding an end to impunity for those behind it. This is all the more impressive because Colombian human rights monitors have paid dearly for their quest with their lives and their security.[130]

State institutions and agencies have also responded to human rights violations in several ways. In different chapters of this report Americas Watch mentions initiatives of the Barco administration, particularly to stem paramilitary violence and drug trafficking, and we comment on their effect on human rights. In the following pages, we discuss other such measures, taken by the Executive Branch or by other state institutions.

A. Constitutional Reform

Most Colombians have high hopes that a lasting solution to their political crisis can be achieved through a Constituent Assembly to be convened at the end of 1990. The Assembly is the product of an initiative by the student movement to include a petition on the ballot in the March 1990 election. It won 2 million votes despite the indifference of the

---

[130] Since January 1987, Human Rights Watch has registered 30 monitors killed and three disappeared in Colombia. Human Rights Watch, *Persecution of Human Rights Monitors*, December 1987, 1988 & 1989 (New York: Human Rights Watch, see various years). Colombia led all other nations in cases of monitors murdered in two of the three reports cited.

political establishment. As a result, the Barco administration included a referendum in the May 27, 1990 presidential election on whether to convene a Constituent Assembly with broad popular representation. The "yes" vote gathered an impressive 5 million, about double the votes cast for Gaviria for President.[131]   On August 1, 1990, an accord was reached among the political parties on the composition of the Constituent Assembly, with 70 members to be chosen in a special election on December 9, 1990. On August 24, 1990, President Gaviria issued Decree 1926 which implemented that accord; the Supreme Court must now rule on the constitutionality of Decree 1926. Many Colombians hope that the *Constituyente* will be a vehicle to provide access to sectors currently excluded from the political system. If that is accomplished, it would go a long way toward strengthening democratic institutions and delegitimizing the recourse to political violence.

B. The Anti-paramilitary Strategy

As stated in Chapters II and III, the actions taken by the Barco administration against paramilitary violence have not yielded the anticipated results. Immediately following the April 1989 decrees, the special elite corps created for this purpose struck a few spectacular blows against self-defense and paramilitary groups in places like San Luis, Antioquia and the outskirts of Bogotá. Those early raids yielded important information about *sicario* schools, communications equipment and training provided by Israeli and British mercenaries. They also resulted in the arrest of individuals charged with the murder of national UP leaders such as Teófilo Forero.[132]   Other police raids at the time uncovered training schools and clandestine graveyards in other parts of the country.

---

[131] CINEP, "Actualidad Colombiana," no. 59, Bogotá, May 17-30, 1990.

[132] Mario Atehortúa Garcés, "Muertos 7 miembros de grupo de autodefensa por la Policía," *El Espectador*, April 6, 1990; "El DAS desmanteló en bogotá una banda de sicarios de 'El Mexicano,'" *El Tiempo*, April 5, 1990; "Complot a sueldo," *El Espectador*, April 6, 1989.

These early actions appeared to have thrown some paramilitary groups into disarray and to have resulted in the capture of some civilian members. But little or nothing was to break the unholy link between self-defense groups and high-ranking military leaders—a factor which, in the opinion of Americas Watch, is decisive in the impunity enjoyed by irregular forces. Early in its term, the Barco administration forced the retirement of Colonel Luis Arsenio Bohórquez Montoya, commander of the Bárbula Battalion in Puerto Boyacá, the heart of narco-paramilitary activity in the Magdalena Medio. This move, technically called *llamado a calificar servicios*, is simply a forced retirement, not even a dishonorable discharge, let alone a criminal investigation and prosecution.

The Bohórquez case reflects a pattern of weak disciplinary response to abuses by security forces. The *Consejería Presidencial para los Derechos Humanos* states that, between April 1989 and January 1990, 36 police officers retired and 63 were "separated." As for the retirements, seven were at the officer's own request, ten by a call to *calificar servicios* and 19 by "decision of the Government." With regard to Army officers, there were 45 retirements and nine separations in the same period. Of the Army retirements, 41 were at the officer's own request, three as a call to *calificar servicios* (including Bohórquez) and one by decision of the government.[133] These statistics do not reveal the reasons behind each decision. In the case of actions against police officers, the majority seem to have been because of corruption, not human rights violations. In the case of Army officers, the high number that requested their own retirement (41 out of 45) suggests that the figure includes many officers who had simply reached retirement age. In this context, "separation" is a disciplinary sanction, whereas "retirement" is not. An independent survey conducted by the Andean Commission of Jurists between April and December 1989 yielded figures almost identical to those of the Consejería. CAJ-SC stressed that none of the Army officers disciplined through dismissal (separation) had a rank higher than Captain.[134]

The initial efforts to combat paramilitarism were not followed through. As noted, when national priorities changed in August 1989,

---

[133] Consejería Presidencial, "Masacres 1988-1989."

[134] CAJ-SC, "Una peligrosa democracia...," p. 5.

these energies were redirected against the Medellín cartel itself, mainly against the inner armed group surrounding Rodríguez Gacha and Escobar.   The fight against the self-defense and paramilitary groups dedicated to political violence, whether or not supported by the drug traffickers, was largely abandoned.   Rodríguez Gacha did command a very active death squad engaged in political violence, and its actions were thwarted by the government's offensive.   But his was not the only paramilitary group, and those acting under notorious paramilitary figures such as Fidel Castaño and Henry Pérez (boss of the Magdalena Medio groups) were clearly independent from "El Mexicano" and have continued to operate.   For example, Luis Rubio, former mayor of Puerto Boyacá, who had been wanted for months as one of the leaders of the notorious Magdalena Medio paramilitary gang ACDEGAM, was briefly jailed on February 24, 1990, having been captured by the Army and handed over to the police.   Three hours after his arrest, a group of armed men freed him from a municipal detention center, without any resistance from the five policemen guarding him.   Three days later, Attorney General Alfonso Gómez Méndez wrote to Minister of Defense Oscar Botero requesting an investigation into why the Army arrested Rubio for "possession of weapons," when it was publicly known that he had warrants of arrest pending against him in other venues for the massacres of Urabá, Mejor Esquina and Punta Coquitos.   The Attorney General also asked for an investigation into why Rubio was taken to a jail in Puerto Boyacá—where no court wanted him—particularly since that is the city where he had been mayor before the Governor dismissed him to stand trial for his role in the massacres.   The transfer suggests a ploy to allow him to escape. Americas Watch is unaware of any investigation into these irregularities.

C. State of Siege Powers

In designing its strategy against political violence, the Barco administration has increasingly resorted to the extraordinary powers granted to the Executive by the state of siege that has been in effect for 34 of the last 40 years.   Most fundamental freedoms have remained available to Colombians, except for occasional and inexcusable restraints on freedom of association, particularly as it affects unions.[135] Guarantees of due process, however, as they apply to certain categories of suspects, have been and continue to be seriously eroded (see Chapter III). Most importantly, the repeated use of executive powers for these measures, to the exclusion of parliamentary debate, have become a feature in Colombian policymaking. Americas Watch understands that there is, indeed, an emergency in Colombia; nonetheless, it seems to us that it would be more appropriate to strengthen regular institutions than to use and create exceptional procedures. In particular, we feel that these momentous decisions should be made with the benefit of democratic debate, rather than by executive *fiat*.

D. Military Areas

By virtue of the state-of-siege powers, President Barco from time to time designated certain zones of conflict to be special military areas, where a military chief with extraordinary powers was appointed. In our 1989 report, we commented on the creation of one such *jefatura militar* in Urabá.[136] In the period covered by the current report, new *jefaturas militares* were created in Pacho and Puerto Boyacá, on September 14, 1989; Envigado, on March 28, 1990; and Bello and La Estrella, suburbs of Medellín, on April 24, 1990. The creation of the military area in Envigado was particularly significant because it was a response to the revelation that the municipal police force had become a death squad engaging in "social cleansing" murders.

The *jefes militares* are given authority to restore public order in these areas, to the detriment of the powers of elected mayors in the realm. They assume command of all local police and security forces, including penitentiary personnel. They have the power to suspend or fire municipal and other civilian officials and to demand cooperation from all government agencies. Though not explicitly included in their powers, in fact the *jefes militares* also have imposed restrictions on freedom of

---

[135] Americas Watch, *The Killings in Colombia*, pp. 80-84.

[136] Ibid. p. 82.

movement and assembly, established roadblocks and identity checks, and generally militarized many aspects of life. This increased control should be expected to diminish the incidence of abductions and murder by paramilitary groups, but in fact, the opposite has been true. Although the Urabá region had been militarized since 1988, it continued in the period under study to be plagued by tragic and frequent killings of peasants, workers, local authorities and court officials.

On July 26, 1990, the Barco administration lifted the *jefaturas* in Envigado, La Estrella and Bello; on July 31, 1990, it terminated the *jefatura* in the ten municipalities of Urabá. Military and civilian officials stated that these measures had been adopted because the objectives of the *jefaturas* had been achieved.[137] At the time of publication of this report, Pacho and Puerto Boyacá, both centers of paramilitary activity, remain under control of *jefaturas militares*.

E. Tribunales de Orden Público

Between 1965 and 1987, civilians accused of insurgency-related crimes were tried by military courts. In 1987, the Supreme Court declared it unconstitutional for military courts to try civilians. The same year, President Barco used his emergency powers to create special courts called Tribunales de Orden Público (Public Order Courts). In our 1989 report, we discussed these new courts and the procedures they followed.[138] These special courts have not only tried cases of political insurgency, but they have also had an important role in the investigation of some of the more notorious human rights violations. Public Order judges have pursued leads linking police and military officers to massacres by paramilitary groups in Segovia and Urabá, and to the murder of an elected official in Sabana de Torres. Those noteworthy achievements, however, do not justify the serious due process problems raised by these courts, especially in their use of evidentiary presumptions

---

[137] Ministers Botero (Defense) and Serpa (Government), quoted respectively in *La Prensa*, August 4, 1990, p. 12, and *El Tiempo*, August 1, 1990, p. 1A.

[138] Americas Watch, *The Killings in Colombia*, p. 94.

against the accused, abbreviated terms for defense motions and the unavailability of release pending trial.[139]

In January 1984, the government created another special jurisdiction, consisting of 60 *juzgados penales especializados*, to deal with crimes related to drug trafficking, kidnapping and extortion.[140] The procedures followed by these courts are very similar to those in Public Order courts.

The 60 Public Order judges (of the 90 that were to be originally appointed) are supervised by one Appellate Court of Public Order, which sits in Bogotá and consists of 12 justices who act in panels of three. In September 1989, a decree authorized the Appellate Court to conceal the identity of the justices voting in each case. Instead, the President (Chief Justice) of the Appellate Court now simply certifies that a decision has been reached and whether there has been a dissenting vote.[141]

This secrecy does not apply to the "first instance" or trial judges of Public Order, even though these are judges who gather evidence and have more direct contact with defendants. If they are threatened, an effort is made to provide them with extra police protection or an armored car, but not much more.[142] The Barco government proposed to create new Public Order courts in particularly violent places such as Turbo and Apartadó in the Urabá region. Dra. Flor Palacios, President of the Appellate Court, told Americas Watch that she did not

---

[139] For a more exhaustive critique, see CAJ-SC, "Sistema Judicial y Derechos Humanos en Colombia," ECOE, Bogotá, 1989, pp. 40.

[140] Law No. 2 of 1984, as amended by Decree 474 of 1988. Article 74 of Law No. 2 established that these courts would exist for six years, after which they would be merged into the regular judiciary. By Decree 2626 of November 16, 1989, however, the Barco administration ordered their existence prolonged for as long as public order remains disturbed and a state of siege is in effect.

[141] The September 1989 decree established the same secrecy procedure for the decisions of the Supreme Court, which rules on the constitutionality of state-of-siege decrees, including the new extradition procedures.

[142] Interview with Dra. Flor Palacios, President of the Appellate Court of Public Order, Bogotá, May 1990.

favor this idea because the violent atmosphere prevailing there would subject those judges to intimidation or would paralyze them; if they were to have their offices in military quarters for protection, they would not be able to investigate possible military involvement in crimes.[143]

Judges of Public Order have been threatened and attacked, particularly when they investigate paramilitary violence. In *The Killings in Colombia*, Americas Watch provided examples of such threats, particularly against Judge Martha Luz González, who had undertaken a commendable investigation in the Urabá case. Judge González's father, Alvaro González Santana, was murdered in Bogotá on May 4, 1989, and his wife was wounded. Judge González had previously been removed from the Urabá case and given a consular post abroad to protect her. Her successor in the Urabá case, Dra. María Helena Díaz Pérez, was murdered with her two bodyguards on July 28, 1989, after several deserters from the Magdalena Medio paramilitary groups had given her additional information on the case.

In addition, Francisco J. Monsalve, another Public Order judge was murdered in Quinchía, Risaralda, on May 20, 1989, when he investigated paramilitary violence in that region. Carlos Valencia, appellate judge of the Superior Tribunal in Bogotá, was murdered on August 16, 1989; and Héctor Jiménez and Mariela Espinosa Arango, both of the Medellín Superior Tribunal, were killed on October 25 and November 1, 1989 respectively. Bernardo Jaramillo Uribe, a Judge of Criminal Instruction (investigatory judge) who was investigating the Segovia massacre, among other important cases, was killed on November 5, 1989 in Medellín. All told, 5 judges were killed in 1988 and 12 in 1989.[144]

---

[143] Ibid.

[144] Consejería Presidencial, "Masacres 1988-1989," pp. 3-4. In a study made for the Center for the Independence of Judges and Lawyers of the International Commission of Jurists, CAJ-SC listed 44 cases of murder and three of disappearances affecting Colombian judges, court officials and lawyers, in the period between June 1989 and June 1990. CAJ-SC, "Jueces y Abogados Perseguidos por el Ejercicio de su Profesión en Colombia: Junio de 1989 and Junio de 1990," Bogotá, August 1990, p. 35.

In the last few months of its term, the Barco government imposed two further due process restrictions on Public Order proceedings. It is now forbidden to make copies of any judicial record of proceedings before this court (defense lawyers can read these materials only in the courthouse). Second, the government repealed a rule which had required that defendants who spend 210 days in preventive detention automatically be set free, with the results that there is now no pressure on judges to complete investigations promptly, and defendants languish indefinitely in jail pending trial.

The government also enacted legislation allowing defendants to testify against their accomplices in return for leniency. Under the new law, if at any time during the proceedings the defendant provides "effective" information, the court must dismiss all charges against him. The law does not define "effective testimony." Information leading to another suspect could be effective without being truthful, and if courts interpret the requirement in that fashion, the new law would provide a powerful incentive to lie, and would consequently raise serious due process concerns.

One problem with the law is that, by requiring the dismissal rather than a reduction of charges, it does not permit courts to distinguish between different levels of culpability. The man who triggered the device that almost took the life of General Maza Márquez (and which killed innocent bystanders), invoked the law to testify against his co-defendants and was, of necessity, freed. At times, other problems have arisen in the application of the law. José Antonio Chaves Fajardo, a participant in the murder of Senator Luis Carlos Galán, revealed names of his accomplices and was released. Chaves was then killed by unknown gunmen, ten days before the first anniversary of Galán's death.[145]

The Dirección Nacional de Instrucción Criminal (DNIC), an administrative body of the judiciary, and the Minister of Justice have authority to change the venue of Public Order courts to any part of the country—a step which they sometimes take as a safety precaution. For example, the La Rochela case (the murder of a Public Order judge and 12 judicial staff in January 1989) has been moved to a court in Pasto. The Segovia case has been inexplicably moved from Medellín to Bogotá

---

[145] *El Tiempo*, August 9, 1990.

(we discuss this move in more detail at the end of this chapter). According to court sources, these changes of venue result in prolonged delays, a matter of heightened concern in light of the mandated incarceration of the defendants pending trial.

Despite the due process shortcuts in the Public Order courts, their efficiency has not improved. Government officials speaking off the record told Americas Watch that on balance the system has not worked. They explained that the protective measures taken have not been enough to shield the Public Order judges from threats and intimidation, and that the magistrates have not availed themselves of expedited procedures for prompt investigations and trials. We would add another reason for failure—the Public Order courts have never enjoyed the military's cooperation when investigations into human rights violations led to officers. Even when judges have ordered the arrest of military officers, they have found it difficult to have their warrants executed. In the Segovia and La Rochela cases, judges seeking to enforce arrest warrants against military officers were compelled to appeal directly to the President for help. At other times, military authorities have informed the court that the officer sought is under arrest in a military installation, but the defendant then continued to attend courses and receive promotions.[146]

In late July 1990, the Public Order Tribunal conducted an evaluation of the judges under its jurisdiction, which resulted in the dismissal of 30 judges for inefficiency and lack of professional competence.[147] In addition, the Gaviria administration has announced that it will combine the Public Order and special courts into a single "specialized jurisdiction," which will hear cases of drug trafficking, anti-terrorism and crimes that cause great commotion in the citizenry. These special judges will live and work in a "citadel" protected by military or security forces, perhaps even within a military installation. The identity of witnesses will be kept confidential, magistrates responsible for

---

[146] Interview with Dra. Palacios, May 1990.

[147] *El Tiempo*, July 31, 1990.

cases will remain anonymous, and "judicial pardon" will be available for those defendants who cooperate with the investigation.[148]

As of this writing, we have not seen the text of the reforms announced by the Gaviria administration. When those measures are enacted, Americas Watch will comment on them as a supplement to this report. In the meantime, we urge the Colombian government to remedy the procedural defects in the existing system so that the new courts operate in strict compliance with internationally recognized standards of due process.

F. The Procuraduría

Under Colombian law, the Procuraduría General de la Nación or Ministerio Público, the office of the Attorney General or Prosecutor General, is independent of all three branches of government. The Attorney General is appointed to a four-year term by the House of Representatives, from a slate proposed by the President. He directs the work of prosecutors at the national and local levels. The office has substantial fact-finding responsibilities and, in the recent past, has played an important role in promoting respect for human rights and the rule of law. The office's effectiveness, however, has depended to a large extent on the personality and dedication of the Procurador.[149] At the time of our last report, Horacio Serpa Uribe had been replaced by Alfonso Gómez Méndez. The new Attorney General has been less outspoken on the issue of human rights than his predecessor, and non-governmental organizations complain that they have less access to him. Nonetheless,

---

[148] *El Espectador*, August 11, 1990, p. 10A.

[149] CAJ-SC, "Sistema Judicial...," p. 236. This important book details the significant work in defense of human rights undertaken by previous Attorneys General Carlos Jiménez Gómez, Carlos Mauro Hoyos and Horacio Serpa Uribe. Americas Watch also noted the role of these jurists in our previous reports on Colombia: *The "MAS" Case in Colombia: Taking on the Death Squads*, July 1983; *The Central-Americanization of Colombia? Human Rights and the Peace Process*, January 1986; *Human Rights in Colombia as President Barco Begins*, September 1986; *The Killings in Colombia*, April 1989.

the office has continued to play a distinguished role in protecting human rights, and Gómez Méndez continues to be the Attorney General in Gaviria's administration.

On January 5, 1989, the Colombian Congress passed Law 21, approving a proposal by then Attorney General Serpa to create an Office of Special Investigations within the Procuraduría. In 1987, the Procuraduría had been deprived of its investigative capacity when the Judicial Police was removed and placed under the supervision of the DNIC.[150] The new Office of Special Investigation (Oficina de Investigaciones Especiales, OIE) has become an important tool for investigating human rights violations, according to Jaime Córdoba, a senior prosecutor and the new Prosecutor-Delegate for Human Rights.[151] The OIE, with a staff of 60 technicians in ballistics, forensic medicine and fingerprints, among others, has become the investigative arm of the Prosecutor-Delegate for Human Rights.

The office of the Prosecutor-Delegate for Human Rights has existed since August 1986, but until 1989 it had no investigative powers. Under Gómez Méndez, the office has been given primary jurisdiction to investigate and prosecute three types of crimes: torture, forced disappearances and genocide. The latter is not construed according to its meaning in international law, but is taken to refer to massacres and multiple homicides when the motive appears to be the elimination of part of a political group.

Córdoba expressed particular concern at the spread of the phenomenon of disappearances. In response, his office seeks not only to identify the immediate perpetrators, but also to prosecute public officials for failing to fulfill important duties, as when a precinct chief allows a detainee to be held without recording him in the appropriate logbook. The penalty for dereliction of duty may be more lenient than for the crime of kidnapping, but we agree with Córdoba that an essential step in the struggle against disappearances is to break the chain of official complicity. We thus applaud as a step in the right direction the effort to

---

[150] CAJ-SC, "Sistema Judicial...," p. 247.

[151] Interview, Bogotá, May 1990.

prosecute military and security agents who look the other way and allow egregious crimes to be committed.

This prosecutorial strategy was followed recently in the notorious case of Pueblo Bello where, as noted, kidnappers driving two large trucks seized 42 men from a town for which the only access was through a 24-hour military roadblock (see Chapter II). On April 30, 1990, the Prosecutor-Delegate for Military Forces filed disciplinary charges against Captain Alvaro Gómez Duque and Lieutenant Néstor Manrique Sierra, of the Voltígeros Battalion, who were in command of a platoon of 12 soldiers at a roadblock that the Pueblo Bello kidnappers had travelled through.

Gómez Méndez has also created a Permanent Commission on Human Rights, chaired by the Attorney General and composed of the Prosecutors-Delegate for Human Rights, for Military Forces, for the National Police and Judicial Police and the Chief of the OIE. The Commission periodically evaluates investigations into violations of human rights. Gómez Méndez has also revitalized a commission created by his predecessor which permitted human rights non-governmental organizations (NGOs) to meet weekly with the Procuraduría. The meetings both allowed the Procuraduría to avail itself of the information and advice of the NGOs and gave the NGOs an opportunity to monitor the Procuraduría's human-rights-related activities. According to Córdoba, the Procuraduría intends to give NGO members a special credential that will authorize them to make inquiries into persons under arrest, to participate in the identification of corpses, and to conduct similar investigations.[152]

Another important breakthrough is a regulatory change in the powers of the prosecutors to obtain official documents. Until recently, the prosecutors were empowered to request information from other agencies only by letter, and were bound by whatever written response they obtained. Under the new rule, prosecutors are empowered to inspect records of all public agencies, including secret military archives, and the evidence thus gathered is admissible in any judicial or disciplinary proceeding. Córdoba told Americas Watch that the Procuraduría is also trying to improve its ability to monitor pre-trial and permanent detention

---

[152] Ibid.

centers, including interrogation centers, on a 24-hour basis. It is also working to prevent human rights violations by educating military and police personnel on human rights matters and by overseeing the mandatory use of the "chart of rights of the detainee" (originally drafted by Attorney General Serpa) by all agents in charge of detentions.[153]

Unfortunately, the record of the Ministerio Público in protecting human rights is tarnished by certain controversial decisions made by Manuel Salvador Betancur, the Prosecutor-Delegate for Military Forces. We refer particularly to Betancur's actions in the cases we discuss later in this chapter, under the headings of Segovia, Gustavo Adolfo Macías Borja and Isidro Caballero. In our last report, we noted the beneficial results of the decision to place civilian jurists in charge of investigations and prosecutions of military officers (previously the Prosecutor-Delegate for the Military Forces had been an active-duty Army officer). However, the actions and rulings in the cases described below raise concerns that those gains will be lost because Betancur's office has tended to follow earlier practices of papering over certain Army abuses.

G. Consejería Presidencial para Derechos Humanos

In November 1987, President Barco created the office of the Presidential Counsellor for Human Rights within the Presidency. The first Counsellor was Alvaro Tirado Mejía, who was replaced in 1989 by Emilio Aljure Nasser. President Gaviria has chosen Jorge Orlando Melo, a distinguished scholar who was most recently Director of the Institute for Political Studies at the National University, as Aljure's successor. The Consejería has become a large and well funded agency, and has succeeded in attracting external funds, including contributions from the United Nations. Because of its proximity to the President, the office enjoys independence from other institutions and a certain stature, but it has no investigative capacity. According to Aljure Nasser, it can only "promote" investigations.[154] On the other hand, the Consejería does have a

---

[153] Ibid.

[154] Interview, Bogotá, May 1990.

professional staff, with specialists in several areas, and a capacity to receive and channel complaints from domestic and international NGOs. That capacity has been enhanced by an institutional arrangement by which the Consejería meets regularly with representatives of different state agencies in an "Inter-Institutional Human Rights Group." The Consejería keeps computerized records of the response to each complaint, and makes this information available to non-governmental groups. It also devotes considerable energy to promoting public awareness of human rights.

The Consejería has also become the government's primary voice in international fora on human rights in Colombia. Both Tirado Mejía and Aljure Nasser appeared frequently before the human rights bodies of the Organization of American States and the United Nations. At the U.N. Human Rights Commission, the Consejero Presidencial made important policy speeches and promoted resolutions on the role of insurgent groups and drug traffickers in human rights violations. It may well be that these appearances abroad were not originally designed to be the Counsellor's main role. Perhaps inevitably, however, this diplomatic role has shaped the attitudes of the Consejería vis-a-vis the domestic front. Both Consejeros have promoted a sophisticated theory of abuses in Colombia; a view which does not deny the existence of abuses, but which finds ways of attributing them to a variety of factors beyond the control of the Colombian government. The drug cartels, of course, are presented as the main culprits, and the government and society of Colombia are portrayed as their victims. Other factors are also blamed, including the rise in street crimes, the guerrillas, and an alleged culture of violence.

The purpose of the Consejería's participation in international fora is, by the office's own admission, to improve Colombia's image abroad. The domestic counterpart of this function is that the Consejería strives at home to attribute responsibility for violence to forces outside the control of the government, again to drug trafficking, subversion and common crime. Significantly, this theory matches the explanation given by military leaders for Colombia's human rights problems.[155] It is an

---

[155] Consejería Presidencial, "Informe anual de labores," Bogotá, January 1989, and "Por la vigencia de los derechos humanos," Imprenta Nacional, Bogotá, September 1988; General Manuel J. Guerrero Pa, "Colombia: objetivo estratégico

explanation that ignores the government's responsibility for the actions and omissions of its agents.

To consider Colombia's human rights violations as an image problem leads inevitably to a tendency to downplay the abuses and to present an overly optimistic view of the steps taken against them. To the Consejería's credit, the information it obtains through its contacts with other government agencies, and shares with NGO's, is unadulterated. However, it presents a picture that resists the Consejería's efforts to blame everyone but the government. Americas Watch believes that the Consejería could be more effective if it used its considerable prestige and resources to present a dispassionate public picture of the cases of human rights violations in Colombia and to speak out in favor of the changes needed to curb abuses.

The Consejería was not conceived as a *defensor del pueblo,* or ombudsman, an institution which would present interesting possibilities for the promotion of human rights in Colombia. The investigative powers of the ombudsman are about the same as those granted the Colombian Consejero: they are empowered to make inquiries at other agencies and to obtain official answers, but typically they lack prosecutorial powers. But most ombudsmen have a potentially very effective tool which the Consejero lacks: the ability to issue public judgments on the behavior of an agency and public recommendations for change. If President Gaviria wants to make the Consejería more effective, he should consider assigning it a more ombudsman-like role. Its judgments and recommendations, if taken seriously by the authorities, could have an important effect on the Colombian human rights situation.

Even without assuming the role of an ombudsman, the presidential advisor could serve as a strong and persuasive moral voice. For several years, both Tirado and Aljure have had access to the media and to large and diverse audiences. They have done much to legitimize the language of human rights and to promote public awareness of these guarantees. But as noted, when it has come to the causes and origins of abuse, their message has been vague, obscuring official responsibility and missing opportunities to offer a moral voice in the government. Such a

---

y los conflictos de baja intensidad," Imprenta Fuerzas Militares, Bogotá, January, 1989; all of them cited in CAJ-SC, "Sistema Judicial...," pp. 240, 243 & 244.

voice is urgently needed inside Colombia. Mr. Melo should—in our view—concentrate on speaking persuasively and forcefully to Colombian authorities and to the Colombian public; the defense of the image of the government in the international arena should be left to diplomats.

H. Access to International Monitors

Americas Watch continued to enjoy access to high-ranking civilian officials in the Colombian government. As in the past, however, we were unsuccessful in obtaining meetings with military authorities.

The ICRC has a delegation in Colombia which regularly visits 26 prisons run by the Ministry of Justice. It also conducts educational programs on international humanitarian law directed to military leaders, members of Congress, and government officials. In addition, it has assisted Colombian non-governmental human rights monitors who campaign for recognition on all sides of the applicability of the laws of war. In 1990, the ICRC provided some humanitarian aid to persons displaced by military operations, and its delegates visited in places where violations had been alleged.

Americas Watch believes that the Colombian government should invite the ICRC to expand its presence in the countryside, as a way of making humanitarian assistance available to victims of war and attempting to decrease the number of breaches of the laws of armed conflict.

As for its work to protect prisoners, it is not enough that the ICRC have access to those who arrive at penitentiary centers. For more than two years, the ICRC has requested access to pretrial detention centers without success. Requests to be given timely notice of the arrest of security detainees, so that they could be interviewed soon after their detention, have also gone unheeded.[156] As we have done in other countries, we urge the Colombian government to grant the ICRC access to all installations where security detainees are held, even for short

---

[156] ICRC, "The ICRC Worldwide 1988," Geneva, Switzerland, 1989, p. 11.

periods, and to provide the notice of arrests that the ICRC has requested.[157] Such access and notice would be an important step towards preventing torture and disappearance, and thus would be a significant demonstration of the Gaviria administration's commitment to curbing those abuses.

I. Status of Important Cases

1. Altos del Portal

On July 6, 1989, the Special Urban Forces (a combined force of the Colombian Army and Navy) attacked an apartment in the Altos del Portal complex in Bogotá. Four men were killed, but the main target, emerald trader Angel Custodio Gaitán Mahecha, miraculously survived. According to court records, the troops had tried to kill him at the instigation of none other than José Gonzalo Rodríguez Gacha, because Gaitán was apparently an informer for the DEA. In December, a military witness revealed that the four victims had been killed after surrender. The Army then formed a court martial [consejo verbal de guerra], and appointed General Farouk Yanine Díaz as prosecutor. On March 9, 1990, the court martial found Navy Captain Gustavo Rojas Moreno (chief of the operation) and Army Captain Jorge Coy Núñez guilty of aggravated homicide and illegal search; Coy and three non-commissioned officers (NCOs) were also found guilty of larceny, and two other NCOs were found guilty of perjury.[158]

2. Urabá

The case concerning the massacres of early 1988 in the La Honduras and La Negra banana farms has not advanced

---

[157] See for example Americas Watch, *Human Rights in Nicaragua 1985 - 1986*, March 1986; *Human Rights in Nicaragua, August 1987 to August 1988*, August 1988; *In Desperate Straits: Human Rights in Peru After a Decade of Democracy and Insurgency*, August 1990.

[158] "Pronta Justicia," *Semana*, March 13, 1990.

much since the Americas Watch report of April 1989. Elsewhere in this chapter, we have mentioned the murder of the father of judge Martha Lucía González, who conducted the initial investigation, and later of judge María Elena Díaz Pérez, who replaced her. No one has been arrested for these murders. Judge González's investigation established that a paramilitary group from the Magdalena Medio region was responsible for the massacres; none of its members, however, have been arrested, except for the brief detention of Luis Rubio, former mayor of Puerto Boyacá, which we also describe in this chapter.

3. Segovia

Judge Martha Luz Hurtado, who had thoroughly investigated the massacre of 43 people in November 1988, is now Regional Chief of the DNIC for Medellín. Other Public Order and Instrucción [investigatory] judges have since gathered evidence on the Segovia massacre; one of them, Bernardo Jaramillo Uribe, was murdered in 1989 (see above). The current mayor of Segovia, Alberto Restrepo, has been threatened: his DAS bodyguards arrested a suspect who was carrying a written threat against Restrepo signed by the paramilitary group Muerte a Revolucionarios del Noreste (MRN), which had committed the November 1988 massacre. The man arrested turned out to be a soldier on active duty with the Bárbula Battalion of Puerto Boyacá.

In spite of these attacks on judges and investigators, a substantial record has been compiled. There has been no change, however, in the legal status of the case since the arrest warrants issued by Judge Hurtado early on, and which we described in our previous report. Lt. Colonel Londoño Tamayo and the other military and police officers and three civilians charged with responsibility for the massacre are in custody. According to the Tribunal of Public Order, in January the officers were in custody in different military units while the civilians were in the Bellavista prison of Medellín. One Army corporal and one Police captain have yet to be apprehended.

We stated in our last report that disciplinary proceedings for "cowardice" against Army Maj. Marco H. Báez Garzón and two captains had been instituted. The Supreme Court had ruled that Londoño et al. were to be tried in civilian courts, while the case against Báez and the captains was assigned to a military court. The disciplinary proceedings have been completed, and the Procurator-Delegate for Military Forces has reversed himself with regards to Báez Garzón. Accepting a motion to reconsider, the Prosecutor-Delegate ruled that the Army's primary responsibility was not to defend the population but to protect military installations; thus, it was not unreasonable for Báez to have reinforced the defenses at Battalion headquarters, even if it meant allowing the killers of 43 civilians to pass unchallenged. The Prosecutor also accepted Báez's reasoning that, to respond effectively, he would have needed information that the people of Segovia had withheld from the Army. We believe this latter argument betrays a blame-the-victim attitude, common in Colombian military leaders, which we would not have expected from a high-ranking prosecutor. In the same ruling, the Prosecutor-Delegate reduced the disciplinary sanction imposed on Police Captain Jorge Eliecer Chacón Lasso, on the grounds that his decision earlier to order his troops to remain inside the police station while the gunmen shot their way through the city was not wholly unjustified, given the magnitude of the attack and Chacón's arrival on the job only 14 days earlier.

Human rights monitors who have looked into the Segovia case believe that, due to pressures on the judges who succeeded Judge Hurtado, other participants in the massacre are not under investigation. For example, Sublieutenant Edgar Fernández Navarro arrested and threatened Segovia activist Eduardo Sierra in October 1988; Sierra was sought out and murdered a few days later during the rampage. Fernández Navarro also organized the fake guerrilla attack that preceded the massacre. In spite of this, he was promoted to Lieutenant on November 28, 1988.

In February 1990, the Ministry of Justice ordered a change of venue in the case, at the request of lawyers for the defense. The case is now before a Public Order judge in Bogotá. The President of the Tribunal of Public Order told Americas Watch that the change of venue would cause a significant delay and was unwarranted. Changes of venue are made for security reasons; in this case, however, there would be no public hearings where the defendants might reasonably be in danger, and if the defendants are at risk in prison, a change of venue does not help them.

The passage of time with no significant progress in the investigation and the unwarranted change of venue raise serious concerns about the outcome of the case.

4. *Sabana de Torres*

Major Oscar Echandía and Captain Luis Ardila, the military officers implicated in the murder of Alvaro Garcés, the UP mayor of Sabana de Torres, Santander, were acquitted on October 3, 1989, by a court martial of the V Brigade, a decision affirmed by the Superior Military Court. The arrest warrant issued against them in February 1989 was never executed because the officers were said to have absconded. As stated in our 1989 report, these officers had planned the murder, given credentials and gun permits to the civilians who killed Garcés, and provided medical attention at the Army's expense for one who was wounded in the attack.

The Procuraduría Delegada, acting at the disciplinary level, ordered the discharge of the two officers. An army spokesman said, in February 1989, that the discharge meant removal from their present posts, not dismissal from the ranks. On November 28, 1989, acting on a motion to reconsider, the Procuraduría reaffirmed its order.[159] Major Echandía was retired "on his own request" on December 30, 1988. Later, in response to the Procuraduría's request, Echandía was discharged "symbolically" on April 7, 1990.[160]

---

[159] Liga Internacional por los Derechos y la Liberación de los Pueblos - Sección Colombiana, "El Camino de la Niebla, Vol. II," Bogotá, 1990, p. 226.

[160] Decrees 2718 and 799, issued by the Ministry of Defense.

5. La Rochela

On January 19, 1989, a paramilitary group in the Magdalena Medio murdered two judges and ten judicial employees who were investigating previous human rights violations.   According to information gathered by the Procuraduría, the massacre of the judicial team was committed by the self-defense group Los Masetos. The Army arrested eleven people on a judge's order in connection with the murders; for security reasons, seven of the detainees were moved to the Bogotá prisons of La Picota and Buen Pastor. In December 1989, seven persons had been indicted [auto de detención], nine had been heard but no charges were filed, and three had been charged but the charges were later dropped.

In May 1990, the DNIC told Americas Watch that eight persons were under detention, including five civilian men and one civilian woman, an Army Lieutenant and an Army Sergeant. All were in Bogotá, but the two military officers were in Army detention centers. The civilians include Alonso de Jesús Baquero Agudelo, alias "Vladimir," a notorious paramilitary leader who is said to appear in the Yair Klein promotion video mentioned in Chapter II of this report.   The DNIC confirmed that three witnesses and one investigator had been murdered since the massacre.[161] To protect the integrity of the investigation, the DNIC removed the case from Santander to the Second Public Order Court in Pasto, in the south of the country. On June 29, 1990, the court convicted five civilians for the crimes of terrorism and multiple murder in La Rochela. "Vladimir" was sentenced to 30 years in prison, the highest penalty allowed in Colombia. Four other civilians were sentenced to prison terms of between 20 and 30 years. Army Lieutenant Luis Enrique Andrade Ortiz and Sergeant Otoniel Hernández were convicted of aiding and abetting terrorist activities, for having provided weapons to the paramilitary group, and were sentenced to five years in prison.

---

[161] Interview with Omar Henry Velasco, Director, Nacional de Instrucción Criminal, Bogotá, May 1990. Peasants from Simacota near La Rochela, also told us about the murder of witnesses.

Previously, a military court (Juzgado de Instrucción Penal Militar No. 126) in the XIV Brigade had dismissed charges [cesación de procedimiento] against Lt. Andrade.[162] The Army had ignored the arrest warrants issued by the Public Order court for these officers, forcing the court to request the President's assistance in obtaining compliance. Sergeant Hernández is incarcerated at the Bogotá Battalion in Pasto. The convicted civilians are also in custody. Lt. Andrade, however, "escaped" from his place of detention. The Pasto judge has ordered a disciplinary investigation of Lieutenant Colonel Rigoberto Tovar Conde, chief of the garrison from which Andrade fled.[163]

6. Palacio de Justicia

Almost five years have passed since the M-19 took over the court building in downtown Bogotá, causing a bloody battle with the police and Army in which several Supreme Court justices died along with scores of civilians and guerrillas. Criminal charges are still pending for the disappearance of persons arrested at the site, and for the decision to disobey an order of the Council of Ministers to suspend the attack on the fourth floor, where the Supreme Court magistrates were being held hostage.[164] The case against 23 M-19 members has been closed under the special pardon law enacted as part of the peace process. The case against Lt. Col. Edilberto Sánchez Rubiano, charged with the disappearance of Irma Franco Pineda and the torture of two students, has died. Although the Supreme Court ruled that civilian and not military courts have jurisdiction (because torture and disappearance are not "acts of duty"), two successive district judges in Bogotá have rejected the case.

---

[162] Liga Internacional por los Derechos y la Liberación de los Pueblos - Sección Colombiana, interview, Bogotá, May 1990.

[163] *El Espectador*, June 16, 1990, p. 11A; *El Tiempo*, June 30, 1990, p. 7A.

[164] Americas Watch, *The Killings in Colombia*, pp. 70-72.

The Procuraduría Delegada for the Military still has disciplinary charges for the same acts pending against Sánchez Rubiano and General Jesús Armando Arias Cabrales, who commanded the operation and is the former Commander of the Army. The defendants have responded to the charges and a final decision is pending. The Supreme Court upheld the decision to prosecute Police General Víctor Alberto Delgado Mallarino for disobeying the order of the Council of Ministers and causing the death of the magistrates. Criminal charges include manslaughter [homicidio culposo]. The case is still pending.

7. *Pardo Leal*

In our 1989 report we pointed out that the case against Rodríguez Gacha for the murder of UP presidential candidate Jaime Pardo Leal had been closed. We also stated that a Ministry of Defense document showed that "El Mejicano" had made calls to Colonel Héctor Julio Ayala Cerón at the Army Cavalry School.[165] This important link between Army officials and the head of a cartel-sponsored paramilitary group remains without serious investigation.

8. *Gustavo Alonso Macías Borja*

In this case, a military patrol had allowed civilians to participate in an official operation, and two of the civilians murdered Macías Borja.[166] The two civilians, the brothers Díaz Cuesta, who were known as Army informants though they had a police record, were arrested and prosecuted. One of the brothers escaped from jail in April 1987 after having given a sworn testimony to a military judge, upon which a decision to exculpate all Army officers was made. In 1988, the Procuraduría Delegada for the armed forces requested the suspension of Captain Carlos Arturo Suárez Bustamante, who had led the patrol. In 1989, after a motion to reconsider, the Procurador

---

[165] Ibid., p. 73.

[166] Ibid., p. 67.

Delegado Manuel S. Betancur changed his mind and acquitted the Captain in the disciplinary proceeding.[167]

9. *Fernando Lalinde*

The only decision by the OAS Inter-American Commission on Human Rights holding that Colombia had violated the American Convention on Human Rights came in the forced disappearance and apparent death of Lalinde.[168] The criminal case for murder is still pending before the 13th Criminal Court of Medellín, though the events took place in October 1984. Disciplinary proceedings were instituted against Captain Jairo Enrique Piñeros Segura and Lt. Samuel Soto Jaimes; on September 12, 1989, the Procuraduría Delegada for military forces declared this action extinguished on statute of limitations grounds. Another two officers implicated have died in unrelated circumstances. Colonel Ayala Cerón (see above for his role in the Pardo Leal case), who was then Commander of the VIII Brigade in Armenia, prevented Mrs. Lalinde from attending the exhumation of the body said to be her son.

10. *Isidro Caballero*

A teacher and union leader in the Magdalena Medio region, Caballero disappeared with María del Carmen Santana on February 7, 1989, in the *vereda* Guaduas, San Alberto, when

---

[167] Liga Internacional port los Derechos y la Liberación de los Pueblos —Sección Colombiana, "El Camino de la Niebla–II," pp. 89 et seq.

[168] Case 9620, Resolution of September 16, 1988; OAS-IACHR, "Annual Report 1987-88," pp. 112 et seq. The Inter-American Commission on Human Rights (IACHR), following the government's suggestion, changed this case from a disappearance to a murder. The alleged murder took place before Colombia's acceptance of the jurisdiction of the Inter-American Court of Human Rights, so the case cannot be submitted to that judicial body. The mother of Fernando Lalinde insists that the government has not proven that Fernando is dead, since the remains exhumed without her presence have been buried in an undisclosed location. Interview, Bogotá, May 1990.

the place was occupied by troops of the Army Mobile Base "Morrison," part of Battalion Santander, V Brigade. The two were apprehended before many eyewitnesses. Applications for *habeas corpus* relief were unsuccessful: all security forces denied holding them. On February 17, 1989, Manuel S. Betancur, Procurador Delegado for the military forces, went by helicopter to the area, searching for the two missing people. He gave advanced notice of his mission by telephone to the chief of the Santander Battalion. A criminal case has been opened before the Second Public Order Court of Valledupar (Cesar), initiated with testimony of eyewitnesses gathered by a municipal ombudswoman [personera] two days after the kidnapping.

As of May 2, 1990, charges and arrest warrants had been issued for the crime of kidnapping against Captain Héctor Alirio Forero Quintero of the Caldas Battalion, as well as against a corporal, a soldier and a civilian. The captain has appealed. The soldier and the civilian are in custody in Valledupar; they are also accused of separate counts of armed robbery. The captain and the corporal are being held in the Army Battalion in Bucaramanga. Military Court No. 26 initiated proceedings in February 1989, but closed them that June because "it was not possible to identify the authors."[169] In another puzzling move, Procurador Betancur has rejected a proposal made by the relatives of the victims that witnesses be shown photographs of the Morrison unit to see if they could identify them. Betancur argued that those photographs were unnecessary because some Army personnel have already been charged. This decision seems to us to neglect a potentially important piece of evidence.

The teachers in the Magdalena Medio have been targeted frequently by paramilitary groups and by the Army. A dossier given by their union to Americas Watch in May 1990 provides

---

[169] Javier Giraldo, S.J., "Una Biopsia a la Impunidad," Sindicato de Educadores de Santander, Barrancabermeja, 1989; Consejería Presidencial para Derechos Humanos, computer printout, 1990; Comisión Regional de Derechos Humanos de Barrancabermeja, interview, May 1990. Americas Watch and CAJ-SC have initiated a case on this matter before the OAS IACHR.

details of teachers forced to abandon positions because of threats; a list of five teachers who have disappeared between 1987 and 1989; and a list of 19 teachers murdered between 1986 and 1990.[170]   Caballero's wife, who has been outspoken in demanding information about her husband, has been threatened.

11. Afranio Parra

A senior M-19 leader and two fellow guerrillas were killed in Bogotá on April 6, 1989, while the M-19 was observing a truce with the government, but before a final agreement had been reached. Policemen captured them while they were using public transportation and murdered them. The case almost caused the peace process to fail. Police agents Félix Pabón Pabón, Vicente Puentes Naranjo and Edilson Cañarte (or Cañarete) were apprehended and charged with the aggravated murder, aggravated larceny and unauthorized possession of weapons. Their trial before Superior Court No. 12 of Bogotá started on September 25, 1990.

The first and last of the examples given above are telling of the attitude of the Colombian government toward the issue of impunity, because in each case there was a motivation beyond punishing human rights abuses which led to a conviction. Altos del Portal and La Rochela are the only cases in which a criminal conviction has been obtained against military officers for their role in a human rights violation. The Army apparently was interested in Altos del Portal because it cannot allow its forces to receive orders from drug kingpins at a time when the United States is poised to provide it with expensive military aid to combat drug trafficking. That the intended victim of the Altos del Portal operation was a DEA informant no doubt stiffened the Army's resolve to punish the officers. In the case of the murder of Afranio Parra, the government's interest in preserving the peace process—and in demonstrating its serious intent to protect the lives of M-19 members—were enough to overcome bureaucratic obstacles and obtain swift apprehension and prosecution.

---

[170] Interview, Barrancabermeja, May 1990.

Human rights monitors in Colombia believe that the complete truth about Altos del Portal has not been allowed to come out, but it is commendable that a serious violation was dealt with promptly. It is also worthy of praise that the investigations and prosecutions for the Afranio Parra and La Rochela cases have been successfully completed, ending in conviction for the perpetrators.

However, these cases stand in stark contrast to the multiple instances in which the chain of command has interfered with and prevented serious investigations into comparable abuses. In La Rochela, with the "escape" of Lieutenant Andrade, only a sergeant is in custody for the Army's role in the murder of court officials. Except for the extraordinary circumstances of Altos del Portal, the Army has yet to allow its officers to be punished for human rights abuses.

VII. The Peace Process

For Colombians sick of incessant political and social bloodshed, the government's peace process represents hope. This hope is embodied in the results of the recent, historic elections, which both represented a partial rejection of traditional political forces and created a new avenue for political participation on the left, the M-19. President Barco's peace initiative, which varied considerably from that of his predecessor, President Betancur, has carried forward the campaign to bring an end to the decades-old insurgency and succeeded, for the moment, in opening a new space in Colombian politics.[171]

However, the path of the Barco peace initiative has not been an easy one. The plan's greatest achievement, the demobilization of the M-19 and its catapult into Colombian politics, was realized after 18 months of arduous negotiations and several crises, including the assassination of the M-19's first presidential candidate, Carlos Pizarro Leongómez. Although the precedent established by the M-19's incorporation into Colombian society has inspired and impelled the ongoing negotiations with other guerrilla groups, most notably the EPL, the future of the Barco initiative, and of the peace process as a whole, is uncertain pending clarification of the approach to be taken by the new President, César Gaviria.

Steps to demobilize the insurgent forces, as contemplated by the Barco initiative, began in January 1989, when the Colombian government signed its first accord with the M-19 guerrillas. The M-19 pledged to maintain the truce begun the previous September and expressed its commitment to reconciliation. Two months later, the government and the M-19 signed an accord agreeing to begin talks in

---

[171] For a detailed account of Barco's peace initiative of September 1988 and the way it differs from Betancur's original peace process, see Americas Watch, *The Killings in Colombia*, pp. 7-16.

April on ending the insurgent movement and incorporating it into civilian life. As a result of these talks, a third accord was signed in June 1989, outlining the procedures for the eventual demobilization of the M-19. Foremost among these were the *mesas de concertación y análisis* [joint commissions for conciliation and analysis], in which representatives of the M-19, the government, the larger political parties and of academic and other social movements, met regularly to discuss the major issues confronting the peace process. The *mesas* were established with the goal of negotiating political compromises in three critical areas: constitutional and electoral reform, public justice and order, and socio-economic issues. The agreements reached by the *mesas* would be considered by the government for implementation by executive decree, legislative proposal, or political agreement.

The next major stage in the M-19's quest for peaceful incorporation came in July 1989, when it and the Colombian government signed an accord for the gradual demobilization of the guerrilla forces by the following December, with the M-19 to participate in elections slated for March and May 1990. A joint declaration issued at the time summed up the conclusions of the *mesas'* deliberations, and assigned them the new task of developing procedures for their implementation. Both the M-19 and the government reaffirmed their commitment to executing these accords in good faith. The agreement, moreover, established a special commission composed of representatives of the M-19 and the government to determine the mechanisms and procedures for the demobilization, disarmament, and eventual incorporation of the M-19 into Colombian society.

The first major crisis in the process came in September 1989, when three M-19 members were assassinated the week before the demobilization commission was to meet for the first time (see Chapter VI). As a result, M-19 commander Carlos Pizarro declared that the talks with the government were in jeopardy, withdrew the M-19 representatives from the *mesas,* and demanded to meet directly with the government to resolve the crisis. The crisis was defused after a series of intense discussions.

After eight years of dialogue with two successive administrations, the M-19 signed an ostensibly final accord with the Barco government on November 2, 1989. The agreement called for total M-19 demobilization by the middle of the following month in exchange for a government-sponsored plan of amnesty and protection for the guerrillas-turned-civilians. This Political Pact for Peace and Democracy [*Pacto Político por la Paz y la Democracia*] was based on the demobilization commission's final report. It presented a framework of basic reforms in the three main areas of discussion in the *mesas*—constitutional and electoral reform, public justice and order, and socio-economic issues. The key provisions of the plan called a nationwide referendum on a proposal to create a special electoral district and new seats in Congress for the M-19, and the convening of a National Constitutional Assembly to discuss other, more profound reforms proposed by the guerrillas.

The plan had to be approved by the traditional political parties of Colombia in a specially convened meeting, before being presented to the Congress for incorporation in the national referendum. Implementation of many of the agreement's key provisions depended on the Congress's adoption of the referendum as a means of reforming the Constitution, a hotly debated issue.

As 1989 drew to a close, the fate of the M-19 accords was again drawn into question, this time by the Congress's refusal in its December session to approve major provisions of the carefully drafted November agreement. The Congress, which reflects the political will of the traditional two political parties, received from the Executive a proposal for a nationwide referendum to convene the Constitutional Assembly and to create special electoral districts. Congress attempted to include the matter of extradition in the referendum; rather than allowing a popular vote on that matter, the Barco administration withdrew its bill, and the proposal for constitutional reform (including the special electoral districts) collapsed. Congress did, however, approve President Barco's amnesty law, which granted pardons to all members of guerrilla groups who embraced the President's peace initiative and laid down their arms. Despite this major setback to the peace initiative, the M-19 continued to disarm while Carlos Pizarro began another round of negotiations with the government to find political alternatives to the defeated measures.[172]

---

[172] "Aprobada ley de indulto para los alzados en armas," *El Espectador*, December 16, 1989.

The amnesty law was, in practice, the only guarantee offered to armed insurgency groups seeking reincorporation into civilian life.[173] Law No. 77 was passed on December 22, 1989 and promulgated by the Executive on January 22, 1990. It benefits those charged with political crimes such as rebellion, sedition, mutiny [*asonada*], extortion, and related transgressions. It requires that the individual applying for amnesty belong to an insurgent group that has unequivocally embraced the peace initiative and committed itself to demobilization and disarmament. The law contemplates three different mechanisms: pardons for those serving sentences, a ban on new criminal proceedings, and an end to pending proceedings. Significantly, it does not apply to homicide outside of combat, terrorism, or other "acts of ferocity or barbarism." To qualify for the amnesty, the Ministry of Justice must certify that the applicant is an M-19 member and that he is on government lists; the court with jurisdiction over the case must then apply the law and, if applicable, order the person's release from custody.

Eighty-six inmates benefitted immediately. The courts also received more than 1,000 petitions, primarily on behalf of M-19 members who had been charged in criminal cases but never apprehended. Human rights lawyers with experience under the amnesty law told Americas Watch that the administrative and judicial process is long and cumbersome. Many had clients in custody who had not revealed that they were M-19 members when arrested, and now have to prove their membership, as well as that the crimes committed had been ordered by the guerrilla group. The Colectivo de Abogados José Alvear Restrepo, a human rights law firm, challenged the constitutionality of the amnesty as being too selective, and because it subjected the will of the individual (to put down arms) to the will of an organization (to adhere to the government's peace process). On July 12, 1990, The Supreme Court ruled against the Colectivo's application and declared Law 77 constitutional.

Despite the signing of the Political Pact and the enactment of the amnesty law, prospects for the peace process were seriously damaged when Congress turned down the reforms agreed upon by the Government and the M-19. Elections were barely two months away and

---

173 "Barco sancionó ley de indulto," *El Tiempo*, December 28, 1989.

the M-19 still possessed no legal means by which to participate. Moreover, even if the M-19 could legally participate, it lacked campaign machinery and even a political platform. In the December talks, the M-19 made the following proposals to salvage the peace process: to postpone the elections, to convene a National Constituent Assembly as a forum for constitutional revision, and to negotiate a new *pacto político*—an agreement among the government, the M-19 and representatives of the political parties and social groups—that would launch a revised peace process. The critical negotiations extended well into 1990.

On March 9, 1990, the government and the M-19 finally reached an agreement which allowed the insurgents at the last minute to participate in congressional and presidential elections. A revised draft of a *pacto político* among the Barco government, the M-19 and the political parties—Liberals, Conservatives and UP—was completed in early February. Its signing, however, was repeatedly postponed while details were ironed out. The thrust of the agreement was straightforward: the M-19 would formally demobilize and disarm within two weeks of signing the pact, in exchange for amnesty and the promise that constitutional reform would be pursued by ordinary and extraordinary means, including a proposed amendment granting the group special treatment in the elections. Paving the way for the signing of the pact, the first M-19 guerrillas were officially pardoned by a Bogotá magistrate under the terms of the new law on February 19, 1990.[174]

President Barco and Carlos Pizarro signed the new agreement on March 9 and hundreds of M-19 militants turned in their remaining arms. The weapons were sent to a smelter to be transformed into a metallic monument to peace. The guerrillas exchanged their fatigues for civilian clothing and a new life in Colombian society.[175] In return for having abandoned armed insurgency, the M-19 received legal recognition and began preparing immediately for its role in the imminent elections as the new political party of the Colombian left. In accordance with its obligations under the agreement, the Barco government in May issued

---

[174] "Indultados dirigentes del M-19," *El Tiempo*, February 20, 1990.

[175] "Colombian Rebels' Arms Go, But Where's Bolívar Sword?" *New York Times*, April 14, 1990.

an executive decree calling a plebiscite on the question of whether to convene a National Constituent Assembly. The Supreme Court ruled this plebiscite constitutional only a few days before the May 27 election. The electorate overwhelmingly voted "yes."

The 1990 Colombian elections will long be remembered as much for the violence unleashed against prominent candidates as for the political inroads made by the nascent Alianza Democrática led by the M-19. In the congressional and mayoral elections held on March 11, Carlos Pizarro entered the Bogotá mayoral contest as a last-minute candidate for the M-19 and garnered a surprisingly strong eight percent of the vote, thereby transforming the three-day-old M-19 into the third largest vote-getter in Colombia.[176]   The AD-M-19 won two mayoral races in San Alberto, Cesar and in Miranda, Cauca, though in both cases the winners were unable to take their posts: one died in a car accident and the other was disqualified because of a pending charge for possession of weapons. Vera Grave was elected as the only AD-M-19 member of the Colombian Congress.

In *The Killings in Colombia*, we noted that for the Colombian left, "peaceful political participation has proven to be more dangerous than armed struggle," a statement made only more true by the recent presidential elections.   The assassination of Galán signaled only the beginning of the political violence against reformist candidates for president. And, as shown previously, on March 22, 1990, the presidential candidate of the UP, Bernardo Jaramillo Ossa, was shot dead by a 15-year-old gunman as he entered Bogotá's El Dorado airport with his family, becoming the 80th UP casualty of 1990, and joining the roughly 1000 other party leaders killed since the UP's inception in 1985. Jaramillo is the second UP presidential candidate to be murdered in as many elections.[177]   The UP emerged as a result of President Betancur's peace process with the FARC, and its decimation has set a

---

[176] Douglas Farah, "Staunch Foe of Traffickers Wins Primary," *Washington Post*, March 13, 1990.

[177] Douglas Farah, "Leftist Politician Killed in Colombia," *Washington Post*, March 23, 1990; James Brooke, "Assassins Wiping Out Colombia Party," *New York Times*, April 8, 1990.

tragic precedent for other aspiring political forces of the left, such as the M-19.

It did not take long for the M-19's impressive debut on the Colombian political stage to be marred by political assassination. After the killing of Jaramillo in March, Carlos Pizarro helped found a coalition of 12 leftist organizations and became its presidential candidate. But a month before the presidential elections, the new leader of the Colombian left was machine-gunned to death aboard an Avianca airliner en route to Barranquilla.[178] As in the case of Jaramillo's killing, it is unclear who ordered the killing of Pizarro (see Chapter IV). Pizarro's murder stands as yet another monument to the impunity of those behind political violence in Colombia. As noted, the government reflexively blamed drug-traffickers for the murders. Numerous communications were received from the cartel and Pablo Escobar denying responsibility for both murders, in contrast to their open admission of responsibility for other killings.[179] Many Colombians believe that Jaramillo and Pizarro were eliminated by extremists on the far right, with the possible participation of military elements.[180] Both were strongly nationalistic, supported dialogue with the narco-traffickers and opposed extradition. Thus, as one journalist observed, "it does not seem likely that the narcos killed [them]. They have the means, without doubt, and maybe even the desire as well. But they did not possess the motive...."[181] In July, however, the Colombian government reaffirmed its theory, and provided

---

[178] Douglas Farah, "Bogotá Candidate Is Assassinated Aboard Airliner," *Washington Post*, April 27, 1990.

[179] "Claims, counterclaims befuddle Colombians," *Miami Herald*, April 29, 1990.

[180] The daily *La Prensa* published on May 2 a report based on intelligence sources which alleged that the assassinations of both Jaramillo and Pizarro had been ordered by extreme rightists linked to Fidel Castaño who had acted independently of the drug cartel.

[181] Antonio Caballero, "La carta robada," *El Espectador*, April 29, 1990; "Bendiciones y Mentiras," *El Espectador*, April 8, 1990.

detailed information to support it, which we describe and comment on in Chapter IV.

Antonio Navarro Wolff, an ex-commander of the M-19, filled the vacuum left by Carlos Pizarro's death, becoming the M-19's second presidential candidate in its two months as a political party. In the May 27 presidential election, he received nearly 13 percent of the vote to finish a surprising third, and defeating the Conservative party candidate.[182] César Gaviria Trujillo, who had replaced Galán as the Liberal candidate, won those elections. According to early results, Navarro Wolff apparently won in the four provincial capitals in which Gaviria trailed, including Barranquilla, Colombia's fourth largest city.[183] President Gaviria fulfilled his campaign promise and appointed Navarro Wolff as Minister of Health.

The hope inspired by the peace process with the M-19 spilled over into negotiations with the other guerrilla movements that remain active in Colombia. The most successful of the recent talks have been those with the EPL, which signed a preliminary agreement with the government in June 1990,[184] similar to the one that eventually led to the disarmament and reintegration of the M-19. On July 24, the government also signed an agreement to begin a peace process with the small PRT, which had operated for about eight years. The agreement was signed in the María Mountains in Bolívar department. In early August, a new round of discussions began, resulting in a pledge by the PRT to give up its weapons by December, a month before the

---

[182] The Social Conservative Party split before the election. The splinter group, Movimiento de Salvación Nacional, finished second. The official Conservative candidate, Rodrigo Lloreda Caicedo, finished fourth behind Navarro Wolff.

[183] Douglas Farah, "Ex-Guerrilla In Colombia's Spotlight," *Washington Post*, June 2, 1990.

[184] "Un primer gran paso en el tortuoso camino a la paz," *El Espectador*, June 10, 1990; "EPL: por el camino de la paz," *El Tiempo*, June 16, 1990.

Constituent Assembly is convened.[185]   Preliminary agreements were reached also with Quintín Lame, an Indian guerrilla group.

On July 27, the government signed a second accord with the EPL in Pueblo Nuevo, Antioquia, officially launching the peace process with Colombia's third largest guerrilla group, despite the refusal of its top leader, Francisco Caraballo, to agree to its terms.[186]   On August 10, about 50 EPL combatants staged a peaceful takeover of the town of Pueblo Rico, Risaralda, where they waited for the government to direct them to a secure place while the negotiations proceeded.[187]   Without the participation of the government, the EPL also initiated contacts with anti-leftist paramilitary groups seeking to reach an understanding.   In mid-August, Ariel Otero, second-in-command of the Magadalena Medio self-defense groups, met with Bernardo Gutiérrez, a member of the EPL high command, in Pueblo Nuevo, Antioquia.[188]   On August 24, Gutiérrez led the EPL delegation that met with Gaviria's new Presidential Advisor for Peace, Jesús Bejarano, in Pueblo Nuevo. By then, Francisco Caraballo had been dismissed as EPL commander.[189]   An important sticking point in these negotiations was the EPL's dissatisfaction with the role assigned to it and other leftist forces in the composition of the Constituent Assembly.   Quintín Lame has expressed its disposition to continue the dialogue with the government, but has not begun the demobilization process because it disagrees with the composition of the Constituent Assembly, which does not include Indian representatives.

In this encouraging context, even the Extraditables seemed to contribute to a climate of peace. In a July 28 statement to the press, they declared a unilateral truce.   While accusing the police of committing massacres while conducting operations against them, they took responsibility for having killed 215 policemen, wounded another 296 and

---

[185] *El Tiempo*, July 25, 1990, August 2, 1990 & August 9, 1990.

[186] *La Prensa*, July 23, 1990; *El Tiempo*, July 28, 1990.

[187] *El Tiempo*, August 11, 1990.

[188] *El Tiempo*, August 20, 1990.

[189] *La Prensa*, August 24, 1990; *El Espectador*, August 25, 1990.

bombed 10 police stations.   They claimed that, as a result of their offensive, more than 400 policemen had resigned.   And they asked that the question of extradition be added to the agenda of the Constituent Assembly.[190] The government replied by questioning the good faith of the proclaimed truce and by rejecting any negotiation with the drug traffickers.   Fidel Castaño, the notorious leader of some of the most dangerous paramilitary groups, also issued a statement from his hiding place, offering to demobilize the Córdoba-based groups if the EPL actually disarmed.[191]

Even with these developments, it must be noted that peace is still distant in Colombia.   The ELN, one of Colombia's two most active guerrilla groups (the other being the FARC), refuses to participate in any peace process.   The FARC continues to proclaim a desire to participate in peace negotiations, but rejects the terms of the Barco peace plan.   In the transition period, the FARC made several overtures to begin peace talks, including an invitation to the government to attend a ceremony in La Uribe—site of its command—to honor its long time leader, Jacobo Arenas, who died of a heart attack in August.   It is said that four FARC fronts in El Meta are ready to break from the parent organization and join the EPL peace process.[192]   The Gaviria government has not responded to the new FARC overtures.   Instead, it has repeatedly stated that the guerrillas, including the FARC and the ELN, can participate in the Constituent Assembly only if they first demobilize.   Conservative Senator Alvaro Leyva Durán, who has championed an alternative peace process, said that the ELN and the FARC have rejected any role in the Constituent Assembly.[193]

While the talks with the M-19 advanced in the summer and fall of 1989, the Coordinadora Guerrillera Simón Bolívar (CGNSB), which is comprised of the EPL, the FARC and the ELN, repeatedly attempted to

---

[190] *La Prensa*, July 28, 1990.

[191] *El Tiempo*, August 1, 1990.

[192] *La Prensa*, August 4, 1990 & August 17, 1990.

[193] *La Prensa*, August 22, 1990.

establish a formal dialogue with the government. However, those attempts were undermined by the FARC's and ELN's persistent refusal to cease all hostilities while negotiations were underway.[194] By September 1989, the Barco government was engaged in intense talks with these insurgent groups in an effort to forge another peace agreement. Hope was expressed that the peace process with the CGNSB would advance along the lines established by the M-19's agreement.[195] Unfortunately, these expectations were premature. The FARC publicly maintained its commitment to negotiating an agreement with the government through the CGNSB, but by early 1990 the ELN had effectively removed itself from the process by launching frequent attacks, including against civilians and economic targets. A major ELN undertaking was a campaign to sabotage the March and May elections, though that factor did not seem to contribute in any significant way to the extremely high abstention rate.[196] In light of the renewed armed struggle, the government announced: "With the ELN, there can be no talks, unfortunately, only persecution."[197]

In January 1990, it appeared that talks with the FARC and the other guerrilla groups were progressing. In a proposal put forth by the FARC at the close of 1989, the guerrilla group offered to reintegrate itself into civilian life as a legitimate political party if the Executive were to call a plebiscite on a National Constituent Assembly for constitutional

---

[194] Enrique Santos Calderón, "Y en qué anda la paz?," *El Tiempo*, June 18, 1989.

[195] "Casa Verde, otra vez," *El Tiempo*, September 8, 1989.

[196] "Fear and apathy may keep Colombians from voting," *Miami Herald*, March 11, 1990. In assessing the ELN's impact on voters, which would have been limited to isolated rural areas, some Colombian observers have discussed "the ELN's 5,000 votes."

[197] "Colombian Marxists Say Time is Right to Step Up Rebel War," *Washington Post*, March 23, 1990; see also "No al diálogo como táctica de guerra: Pardo," *El Espectador*, January 19, 1990, in which the president's principal negotiator in the peace process, Rafael Pardo, stated that the government will not engage in dialogue unless the parties demonstrate their desire to achieve peace by beginning an effective cease-fire.

reform. Unfortunately, the FARC's refusal to cease all hostilities and to abide by other prerequisites to negotiation established by the government prompted the government to break off talks in early 1990 and to demand that the FARC clarify once and for all its objectives before a "climate of confidence" could be established and the talks renewed.[198]   Because of the FARC's opposition to the government's terms for negotiating an agreement, some Colombian experts on the insurgency believe that the FARC, like the ELN, will continue fighting for many years to come.[199]

The Gaviria administration has ratified and adopted the Barco peace plan, and does not appear ready to introduce any significant adjustments. Rafael Pardo, the Presidential Counsellor for Peace who negotiated the M-19 agreement, has been appointed Presidential Counsellor for Security, a new position designed to coordinate the President's policies governing the armed and security forces in their counterinsurgency and drug interdiction efforts. Jesús Antonio Bejarano, the new Presidential Counsellor for Peace, was a senior member of Mr. Pardo's team. Bejarano will continue to manage the PNR, which is one of the tools of the peace process. On drug trafficking and paramilitary groups, the Gaviria administration also seems to have continued Barco's policies: ostensibly any suggestion of negotiation is rejected, but the government responds to unilateral gestures with gestures of its own. It is significant, for example, that the military *jefaturas* in the suburbs of Medellín, designed to concentrate the military and police effort against the drug cartel, have been lifted.[200]   The decision to end them came in late July 1990 on the heels of the unilateral truce declared by the Extraditables.

---

[198] "Reglas de juego para diálogo con la FARC, fija el Gobierno," *El Espectador*, April 20, 1990.

[199] "Colombian rebels seen as survivors," *Miami Herald*, March 10, 1990. Colombian observers have expressed some hope that the death of Jacobo Arenas, long-time leader of the FARC, may signal some opportunity for a change in attitude toward the peace process.

[200] The other *jefatura* that has been ended is in the Urabá region, which is the site of most EPL activity.

More recently, the Gaviria administration seemed to respond to the relative peace with the drug traffickers by offering reduced sentences and immunity from extradition in exchange for surrender and cooperation (See Chapter III). On the other hand, the government has refused to alter other important elements of the Barco drug policy. Gaviria has ratified General Miguel Maza Márquez as head of DAS and Colonel Oscar Eduardo Peláez Carmona as head of DIJIN, both of whom have incurred the hostility of the Medellín cartel because of alleged abuses committed by forces under their command.

The opening with the EPL, Quintín Lame and PRT has given the peace process renewed vigor. More important, the Constituent Assembly offers hope that fundamental questions of political participation may be addressed. If the political system provides an opening for sectors of society that now feel disenfranchised, the Assembly will have removed a historic cause of political violence. In the meantime, the current course seems to leave no room for serious negotiations with the largest guerrilla groups. The ELN is probably not interested in peace under any circumstance, but in any event, an agreement with the FARC would be extremely important, not only because of the FARC's size and military might, but also because of its undeniable social base among large sectors of the Colombian poor, and its influence and contacts with unarmed political organizations.

VIII. U.S. Policy

In the United States, the human rights tragedy of Colombia has been overshadowed by—and often confused with—the Medellín cartel's violent response to President Barco's initiatives to bring them to justice and to extradite them to the United States. As explained in Chapter II, drug traffickers are involved in political violence through the support they give to paramilitary groups. In addition, the cartels use violence in their regular criminal transactions and in reprisals against judges, prosecutors and government officials. However, in their capacity as financiers, leaders and suppliers of the paramilitary groups, the drug kingpins enjoy an important measure of cooperation from well-placed and high-ranking agents of the state, especially among the military. At the same time, paramilitary groups are neither "wholly owned" nor are they completely dependent on the drug cartels. Other powerful economic and social interests use paramilitary violence for their own ends. These multiple sources of violence in Colombia, unfortunately, are lost on the Bush administration, which in 1989 launched an ambitious plan to support President Barco's "war on drug traffickers" without any comparable concern over abuses sponsored or tolerated by state forces.

The Bush plan known as the "Andean Initiative," was announced on September 5, 1989, after the murder of Galán had raised the stakes of the confrontation between the Colombian government and the cartels. Only the general outline of the Bush plan was announced in September; for several months, the details were negotiated with the U.S. Congress, largely out of public view. On November 22, Congress approved the International Narcotics Control Act of 1989; President Bush signed it into law on December 13, 1989.

Under the Act, the Bush administration intends, between 1990 and 1994, to spend over $2 billion on military aid, economic aid and law enforcement assistance for Colombia, Peru and Bolivia. As proposed in 1989, Colombia would receive approximately $382 million in military and police aid and $204 million in economic aid during the five-year plan. For fiscal years 1989 and 1990, however, all of the new assistance for Colombia has consisted of military aid, including weapons, training and advice, and the amounts have grown steadily in the months since the Bush plan was announced. In August 1989, President Bush used his authority to "drawdown" defense stockpiles to release $65 million in military aid and equipment to Colombia. This was the largest amount ever drawn from the stockpiles, which are maintained to confront emergency military crises. In 1989, Colombia received a total of $73.6 million in military aid (including the $65 million drawdown), which represents more military aid in one year than in the 20 preceding years combined, all designed to help the Colombian Army and police fight the druglords.

In 1990, the administration announced to Congress its intention to drawdown new funds for Colombia from the stockpile, this time in the amount of $20 million in "equipment and services."[194] For fiscal year 1990, the Bush administration proposed to give Colombia $80 million in military and police aid for narcotics control (this includes the $20 million drawdown discussed above). In addition, in FY90 Colombia will receive $30.9 million in military aid originally set aside for Peru but rejected by President Alberto Fujimori. (This amount apparently will be subtracted from Colombia's FY91 counternarcotics assistance.) Therefore, Colombia will receive over $110 million in military and law enforcement assistance

---

[194] The assistance is described as supplemental to the 1989 drawdown. It is to be distributed as follows: $5 million to the National Police (cited as "the first priority for Colombia") and $15 million for the Colombian Air Force, Army and Marine Corps. The items to be donated are described as: individual troop and aviator equipment, UH-1H helicopter spare parts and support, critical aircraft spare parts, strategic and tactical communications, "tactical intelligence," radar-site security (weapons and ammunition), spare parts and support for C-130, UH-60 and UH-1H aircraft, "armament components," M-79/50 CAL machine guns and ammunition, and "Riverine weapons." Letter to Dante Fascell, Chairman, House Committee on Foreign Affairs, from Janet G. Mullins, Assistant Secretary for Legislative Affairs, Department of State, August 10, 1990. The drawdowns in FY89 and FY90 are both in addition to the military aid to Colombia approved in the five-year plan.

in FY90. For FY91, the administration requested $60.5 million in military aid and an additional $20 million in police aid.

A central element in the Barco strategy, inserted at U.S. insistence, was the extradition of drug kingpins to the United States. The United States thus was directly linked to the success of the strategy, as well as to the controversy surrounding extradition and to the troublesome reports of torture and disappearance of persons arrested for extradition. Many Colombians oppose extradition in general on grounds of national sovereignty; others oppose this particular extradition decree because it fails to provide for judicial review and because it was enacted without debate in Congress (see Chapter III).

The Andean Initiative plays well to the U.S. public, understandably supportive of what sounds like a tough approach to the drug trafficking that has immersed American cities in unprecedented violence. Whether the plan will stop the flow of drugs is an open question, and one which lies outside the mandate of Americas Watch as a human rights organization.[195] We are concerned, however, with the effect on human rights of the administration's plans to combat drug traffic. Our concerns are heightened by the administration's declaration of "war" that is, its largely military response to a law enforcement, if not a social problem.

Many Colombian voices have been raised to insist that other, non-military solutions be given greater weight, including more effective ways of reducing consumption and drug dependency in the U.S. market. President Bush's message of September 5, 1989 made reference to the need to control the export of chemicals used to refine coca leaves, and to revise banking-secrecy regulations so that drug-trafficking proceeds are not so easily laundered in Florida banks. These issues were also raised

---

[195] As an illustration of the rising controversy on the effectiveness of the Bush administration policy, a recent report by the Committee on Government Operations of the U.S. House of Representatives (see footnote 66) harshly criticized the DEA for its failure to reduce coca cultivation and processing in Peru and Bolivia. The report praised Colombia for its successful interdiction efforts, pointing out that U.S. success was achieved despite the absence of "Operation Snowcap" DEA agents in Colombia. The report also noted that the National Police is responsible for 90 percent of all drug seizures in Colombia, yet it received only 16 percent of the initial $65 million in U.S. military aid.

by the Latin American presidents at the February 1990 summit in Cartagena, and President Bush appeared to agree in principle that they needed to be addressed. But for now, at least, the U.S. government is making no effort to cover these gaps in its policy.

Moreover, the Bush Administration has shown no interest in restricting the private export of weapons to Colombia. Paramilitary groups and cartel thugs buy assault rifles and semi-automatic guns of all sorts in the United States, where the gun lobby effectively prevents any meaningful restriction on their sale. It appears that a large number of the Chinese-made AK-47 assault rifles that were sold by the thousands in the United States have made their way to the cartels.

In response to public outcry over the killing of schoolchildren in California, President Bush restricted the sale of imported automatic weapons, but he refused to institute any controls on semi-automatic weapons and on any weapon manufactured in the United States. Nor are there any plans to restrict the export of guns. This attitude allows the drug cartels to build effective defenses against Colombian law-enforcement efforts, and gives paramilitary groups the tools to continue political murder. The administration should express its support for U.S. Congressional efforts to control the flow of weapons to Colombia.

The International Narcotics Control Act of 1989 (PL 101-231) states that one of the three purposes of the military aid it authorizes is to:

> strengthen respect for internationally recognized human rights and the rule of law in efforts to control illicit narcotics production and trafficking.

The Act also stipulates that assistance may be provided only so long as:

> the law enforcement agencies of that country do not engage in a consistent pattern of gross violations of internationally recognized human rights [as defined in Section 502B(d)(1) of the Foreign Assistance Act of 1961 (22 USC 2304(d)(1))].

In addition, the Act includes a requirement to report on human rights:

Section 3(g) Reports on Human Rights Situation: Section 502B(c) of the Foreign Assistance Act of 1961 (22 USC 2304(c)), relating to country-specific human rights reports upon the request of the foreign affairs committees applies with respect to countries for which assistance authorized by this section is proposed or being provided.

This means that, if requested by the appropriate Congressional committee, the administration would be required to report whether the recipients of aid are engaged in a consistent   pattern of gross violations of human rights; if such a pattern is found, the aid will cease.

The requirements of Section 502B, however, have not prevented the administration from providing aid to some of the worst violators in the Western Hemisphere, and there is little reason to believe that its impact will be any different in the Andean countries. The Colombian and Peruvian armed and security forces, the intended recipients of most of this aid, are responsible for or complicit in some of the worst violations taking place today in the Americas, the conflicts in Central America included. The behavior of those forces in counterinsurgency and internal-security operations should make them ineligible for aid, whatever their behavior in drug-interdiction operations. Moreover, as documented in Chapter III, even in anti-trafficking operations, there is growing evidence of abuses.

The administration's policy, and the intent of Congress in supporting it, may be to enlist Colombia's assistance in stopping the flow of cocaine to the United States, but it is having little effect in convincing Colombian generals to restrict the aid to that use. As in Peru, the Colombian high command is more interested in pursuing counter-insurgency operations, as it has for decades, than in taking on the newfound drug-trafficking enemy. Naturally, the generals can be expected to use the new bonanza of U.S. military aid in accordance with their own priorities.

A recent report of a U.S. Congressional committee recorded interviews with Colombia's top military leaders in which they described "Operation Tri-Color 90," a major three-year offensive against the insurgents launched by the Colombian Army on April 1, 1990. They said that $38.5 of the $40.3 million in military assistance appropriated in

FY90 as part of the U.S. Andean Initiative will provide most of the logistical support for this operation.[196]

The Congressional report provides strong evidence that the aid sent for anti-narcotics operations is actually being used to support and expand the Colombian military's counterinsurgency effort. The U.S. government is thereby becoming involved in an operation that has a long history of "dirty war" tactics and of gross disregard for the laws of war. We believe that finding the security forces responsible for such abuses is a direct violation of the laws governing U.S. foreign assistance, which at the very least merits serious, open debate and review.

Secretary William Bennett, the Administration's former "drug czar," offered assurances that aid will not be given to human rights violators. That vow, however, seems impossible to keep in light of the intended beneficiaries of the program. This and earlier Americas Watch reports have shown the Colombian armed forces to engage in a systematic pattern of violations of the laws of war.

Moreover, Bennett asked Congress to waive the prohibition on aid to police forces which has been in place since the 1970s. In a compromise, Congress approved the $125 million package but ordered that no more than 10 percent of the money spent in each country could go to police forces. In this fashion, restrictions that have effectively prevented the United States military from becoming linked to police practices of torture, disappearance and execution are quickly being swept aside. Latin American police bodies, whether under democratic or dictatorial governments, continue to use torture as a standard interrogation technique. The current drug crisis seems to be providing

---

[196] U.S. House of Representatives, Committee on Government Operations, *Stopping the Flow of Cocaine with Operation Snowcap: Is It Working?*, (House Report 101-673), August 14, 1990, pp 83-84. The report added: "When asked by the subcommittee staff to explain how a major military operation in an area not known for its narcotics production could advance the antinarcotics goals of either country, the military representatives stated that if processing facilities were located during the operation they would be destroyed."

the excuse to abandon a policy that was soundly based on ethical and practical grounds.[197]

In similar fashion, the rush to provide aid to the Colombian Army and police ignores the unholy alliance that exists between the Medellín cartel and certain high-ranking officers. Born out of corruption, the alliance, as noted, also has an ideological component: they combat the guerrillas and their perceived allies among trade unions, leftist parties, community organizations and human rights groups. Fixated on the cartels' attacks on Establishment politicians and judges, the Bush Administration has overlooked this alliance, with the danger that its aid will strengthen the most anti-democratic elements in the Army and fuel the "dirty war."

The Bush administration has simply brushed aside these objections to its aid package, suggesting increasingly that it is determined to press ahead with military and police aid regardless of the troublesome human rights behavior of the Colombian armed forces. Despite Bennett's assurances, the administration seems to regard legal restrictions on aid to abusive forces as nothing more than bureaucratic hurdles that can be mounted with "assurances" of a purely rhetorical nature.

We believe that the only reasonable construction of Section 502B of the Foreign Assistance Act of 1961 and of the International Narcotics Control Act of 1989 is that the Colombian military and police are ineligible to receive aid because of their current abusive practices. To receive that aid, they must demonstrate a clear end to those practices. Instead, they have refused even to acknowledge them. If Congress is willing to countenance this skirting of the law, it should at least impose more specific conditions on the aid now flowing to minimize its support of abusive practices. Among possible conditions, we suggest that the Colombian government should:

---

[197] Assistance provided by the DEA or the FBI does not require a waiver of Section 660 of the Foreign Assistance Act of 1961. However, Congress must grant a waiver in order for the U.S. military to provide police training. In this way, Congress is able to limit some of the police assistance.

—end the involvement of members of the armed forces and law enforcement agencies in political violence and human rights abuses;

—vigorously prosecute all persons who have been charged with human rights abuses;

—provide an adequate and timely registry of those persons detained by all instrumentalities of government so that family members of detained persons may be notified of the whereabouts of their relatives;

—provide a full accounting of any persons who have disappeared while in official custody;

—grant the International Committee of the Red Cross access to all places of detention, including police stations and army barracks, where persons accused of security-related offense are held;

—demonstrate that the government has effective control over police and military operations related to counternarcotics and counterinsurgency activities.

The Colombian government deserves help in fighting the cartels. Military aid, however, can and should be conditioned on an effort to sever the unholy alliance that has contributed to the continuing Colombian bloodbath. The infusion of vast amounts of aid could help promote human rights, but only if the Bush administration is willing to use it as leverage to encourage the democratic institutions of Colombia to investigate the paramilitary groups thoroughly, to punish those officers who have contributed to political violence, and to drive the cartels' military allies out of the armed forces. Unfortunately, the Bush administration has yet to show any interest in pursuing these ends.

Appendix

The following is a communiqué from the Government of Colombia responding to the preceding report. It first appeared as an article entitled "'Américas Watch desconoce la acción del Gobierno,'" ["'Americas Watch ignores government action'"] in the October 23, 1990 issue of *El Espectador*. (Translation by Americas Watch.)

The Office of the Presidential Counselor on Human Rights has quickly reviewed the new Americas Watch report. This report should be considered an important contribution to the debate on human rights in Colombia and deserves to be carefully studied by all citizens. In pursuing its mission, Americas Watch presents a balanced account of human rights abuses attributed to both state and guerrilla forces, and attempts to capture the complexity of the violence in Colombia. Also, it recognizes how, in spite of the challenges presented by organized crime, it has been possible to maintain a democracy that permits the almost unlimited enjoyment of basic civil rights. And, it gives credit to the principal state agencies for their efforts in guaranteeing the defense of human rights.

However, their analysis of the facts leads Americas Watch to believe that a high degree of cooperation between government agents and drug-traffickers exists, and also that there is a policy of systematic human rights violations by high government officials and commanding officers of the Armed Forces. The Counselor's Office considers these claims to be unjustified generalizations, based on a few real cases, many of which took place during a time in Colombia very different from the present. The cases mentioned by Americas Watch do not take into account the dominant trends of government policy and action, including those of all its agencies and branches. Because of that, the report minimizes the efforts of the previous [Barco] administration and of high military and police authorities against corruption and against the ties between some government officials and drug-traffickers.

Also, the report does not take into account the new climate created in the country by the convocation of a new National Constituent Assembly. The Assembly opens wide the prospect of active participation by all domestic sectors in defining the foundations of our political structure. This new environment has been reinforced as well by the prospect of a negotiated solution to the conflict with the guerrilla groups. Over the past few weeks, this climate has also contributed to a clear decrease in political violence, which we hope to consolidate gradually.

Americas Watch proposes a number of legal recommendations to improve the human rights situation in the country. These proposals currently are being discussed by different governmental bodies in order to define their eventual adoption into law, either through state of siege decrees, legislative bills, or in some cases, the new Constitutional Charter. The government has already adopted other policies suggested by Americas Watch, such as a new peace proposal and the announcement of an objective national report on human rights, both of which came before the release of the Americas Watch report.

In spite of these coincidences, the previously mentioned disparities indicate that a much wider discussion of both the events Americas Watch mentions, as well as the general conclusions they reach, is warranted. In a few days, the Counselor's Office will address this issue in a detailed report that should contribute to a more precise analysis of the problem, and also to help Colombians defend their fundamental rights with increased vigor.

Jorge Orlando Melo, Presidential Counselor on Human Rights.